T0106253

RIVER OF NINE DRAGONS

By: John Richardson

The Ranger's Prayer

Isaiah 6: 8

*Then I heard the voice of the Lord
saying, "Whom shall I send?
And who will go for us?"
And I said, "Here am I. Send me!"*

SUA~SPONTE
OF THE OWN ACCORD

ISBN: 978-1-4269-6521-0 (sc)
ISBN: 978-1-4269-6530-2 (e)

Trafford rev. 04/16/2011

 www.trafford.com

North America & international
toll-free: 1 888 232 4444 (USA & Canada)
phone: 250 383 6864 ♦ fax: 812 355 4082

NOVELS BY
JOHN RICHARDSON

RIVER OF NINE DRAGONS

HEAVENS ALTER

RANGERS DECLARES WAR
ON ALABAMA
COMING SOON

FROM THIS VALLEY
COMING SOON

BASED IN PART ON
TRUE EVENTS ~ EXACT
LOCALS, DATES AND NAMES
WERE CHANGED
TO PROTECT THE INNOCENT

~ ~ ~

U.S. ARMY RANGERS
BUSHMASTERS
OPERATES UNDER OCSEC
(OPERATIONAL SECURITY)
NO INFORMATION, IS DISCLOSED CON-
CERNING MISSIONS
ASSIGNED OR COMPLETED

For The Following
~ Lesley ~
1945 – 2007
~ Randy ~
1948– 2010
~ To SSG Jack Beair - The
Bravest Man I've ever Known ~
1932 ~ 2009
~ Jeanne Giaier ~
~ Mary Drysdale ~
~ Don Wilkerson ~
~ Bob Wilkerson ~
~ Jimmy Johnson ~
And to the Women and
Men at SobSquad.net
Also to Dr. Cynthia Glasson
And her wonderful staff.
The Doctor's & Nursing
Staff of the Veterans Hospital
&
The University Hospital in
Ann Arbor Michigan for
Keeping my Old Ass Alive

You came Warrior.
To Be Warrior.
Only through Being
Can you effect Change.
Realize then Warrior,
The Job you do.
The Burden you chose to bear,
To change our Warrior World.
Leave your guilt then
In the rice paddies, with the blood.
That was shed on your journey
And let Mother Earth
Heal herself with it.
As you write your story,
Heart exposed through your words.
Reaching out to those who need
To hear them.,
~ Jeanne Giaier ~

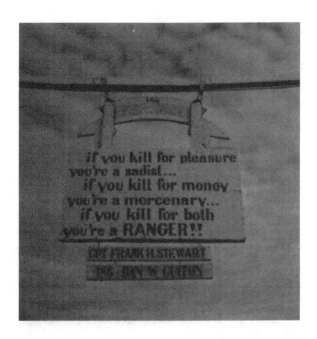

THE RANGER CREED

Recognizing that I volunteered as a Ranger, fully knowing the hazards of my chosen profession, I will always endeavor to uphold the prestige, honor, and high esprit de corps of the Rangers.

Acknowledging the fact that a Ranger is a more elite soldier who arrives at the cutting edge of battle by land, sea, or air, I accept the fact that as a Ranger my country expects me to move further, faster, and fight harder than any other soldier.

Never shall I fail my comrades. I will always keep myself mentally alert, physically strong, and morally straight and I will shoulder more than my share of the task whatever it may be, one hundred percent and then some.

Gallantly will I show the world that I am especially selected and well-trained soldier? My courtesy to superior officers, neatness of dress, and care of equipment shall set the example for others to follow.

Energetically will I meet the enemies of my country. I shall defeat them on the field of battle for I am better trained and will fight with all my might. Surrender is not a Ranger word. I will never leave a fallen comrade to fall into the hands of the enemy and under no circumstances will I ever embarrass my country.

Readily will I display the intestinal fortitude required to fight on to the Ranger objective and complete the mission, though I be the lone survivor.

Origin of The
Best of the Best
The United States Army Elite Rangers

It was during the revolutionary war of 1771. General George Washington ordered Lieutenant Colonel Thomas Knowlton to select an elite group of men for reconnaissance missions. This unit was, known as Knowlton's Rangers. Knowlton's Rangers was the first official Ranger unit for the United States of America. The Elite Rangers is the father of the modern day Special Forces, and Delta Force...

* * * *

Origin of the U.S.M.C
The United States Marine Corp

Captain Samuel Nicholas formed two battalions of Continental Marines on 10 November 1775 in Philadelphia as naval infantry. Origin of the Marine Corps...

Force
Reconnaissance

Marine Corps Force Reconnaissance was conceived in 1954, at Marine Base Camp Pendleton, outside of San Diego. The precursor of Force Recon was the World War II. Captain James L Jones commanded the Amphibious Reconnaissance Battalion...

* * * *

Origin of The Delta Force

Origin of The Delta Force. This unit was, created to combat increasing hostage situations involving terrorist, involving Highjacking of airplanes and/or vehicles as well as other hostage situations. U. S. Army Colonel Charles Beckwith suggested this to the DOD. A small, tactical team capable of responding with quick and deadly force, once approved, Col. Beckwith in 1977 assembled the force and recruited from the Green Berets, the Army Rangers and the Airborne Divisions...

* * * *

Origin of the Special Forces

Origin of the Special Forces – 1950 - May 1954.The French Army was, defeated by the Viet Minh, the Communist-supported Vietnam Independence League at Dien Bien Phu.During those years the U.S. Army Special Forces came into existence...

* * * *

Origin of The Green Beret

In 1953 Special Forces Maj. Herbert Brucker originally designated The Green Beret head cover. The beginnings of the Army Special Forces can be traced all the way back to a small contingent of Confederate Civil War soldiers led by Col. John Mosby. The soldiers staged raids in a manner that more resembles the Army Rangers...

* * * *

The Origins of the Navy SEALS

The origins of the Navy SEALS go back to World War II. Amphibious Scout and Raider School was established in 1942...

* * * *

Origins of Hoooorah

No one actually knows. It's like the word 'Shit'. Who created that word? My guess is that Noah said it when he struck a digit while constructing the Ark.

Ho Chí Minh has been, credited with marrying nationalism to communism, as well as perfecting the deadly art of guerrilla warfare in a pursuit of a "New World Order"
UPI Radio

Ho Chí Minh fashioned the Democratic Republic of Vietnam in 1945 writing a declaration of independence that stated, 'All men are created equal; they are endowed by their Creator with certain inalienable rights; among these are Life, Liberty, and the Pursuit of Happiness.'

During a cruel take over after Ho became president of North Vietnam, an estimated 50,000 North Vietnam citizens were murdered, At that point, between 50,000 to 100,000 were Imprisoned. Freedom of speech was restricted. Ho Chí Minh, unlike United States was the final word. His heart and soul was committed to unifying North Vietnam with South Vietnam...
UPI Radio

CONTENTS

Teddy Pendergrass, American R&B and soul singer died today...
01/13/10
http://en.wikipedia.org/wiki/2010

CHAPTER ONE

PRESENT DAY: I awoke from a nightmare triggered by yet another thunderstorm. Therefore, I sit here watching and listening to the newscaster on Channel 4 as he gives out the latest American death toll in Iraq. Of soldiers many people are saying should not be over there in the first place.

I cannot help it. I cannot stop it. My mind drifts back to another place, back to the jungles of Southeast Asia, a vacation spot provided to some of us by way of the U.S. Government. Better known as South Vietnam, to a time when the American people were, divided over another unpopular war.

Because of it, my soul's plagued by dreams of the faces of my enemy. Whose lives I had taken so long ago, their spirits tormenting me every waken minute of every day. In my latest dream, rich red blood drips from the ceiling, and oozes out of the walls moving like thick gravy toward the floor. The floor is soaked with the life-giving substance, moving like course water toward the hallway. The closet doors take on a life of their own, playing like a horror movie, opening and closing at will, revealing a different face, or faces with each unfolding.

Like so many nights before, I get up sweating and gasping for air as I leave the bed for my wheelchair. Rolling into the living room, I frantically search for the Prozac and a bottle of Jack to wash the pills down, all in the hopes of relieving my mental anguish. All the same, even awake I still see the faces of the past, because my mind resides there, there in the past, there in the fog and rain, there for a purpose, there with a mission.

It's been said that time heals everything, and that may be true for some people. However, for me, the only thing that has changed is, I'm older now with a body that seems to be reaching its end, while my mind is still stuck at twenty-five.

No idea how long I have left, maybe I am just growing tired, or running out of energy, I'm not sure. The doctors say that my disease, CIDP (Chronic Inflammatory Demyelinating Poly-Neauropathy) is a disease that attacks the nerves and the muscles in the body, for which there is treatment, but no cure. Not worried about it, because if my disease does take my life. I know that death comes with the natural order of things. I'm not in a hurry to see what's next, but I'm not afraid of it either. Maybe it's God's way of punishing me for what I've done. By trapping me in a body that no longer works as it once did, if so, I must admit, it seems a fitting end for my sins.

The first time I heard this phrase, I thought that I was in love. I've heard the words spoken only once, but I think of them a lot. 'Toi pham mà Hiên đuong se không đe lai không bi trung phat.' (Crimes that Heaven will not leave, unpunished).

I refuse to blame God for my undoing, and for actions that were committed by my hands. When I humble myself before Him, asking for His forgiveness, I find that the words do comfort me, but only for a short time. I say for a short time, because eventually. The thoughts and dreams slowly begin creeping back in.

Presently, the rain is coming down in earnest outside, pounding hard against the front windows. I watch as the water lit by the cracking white streaks of lightening run in small waterfalls down the glass. Splattering against the brick, seal beneath the window frame. Pooling on the ground, and absent of the redness of blood of times past.

'Mua' is a simple word, it means rain in Vietnamese, and the word should be Hell when it comes to describing the rains in Vietnam. Some say Monsoon describes it best, not so. It's a punishing torrential rain that brutality hammered down our bodies with heavy marble size missiles. Rains that was far more foreboding and haunting than they could ever be here at home, heavy, dark and gray rain, thick, and almost black at times.

My mind travels back to 17 November 1965. We were a small six-man team of US Army Rangers. Members of a Special Covert Black Ops Unit, Surrender, or Bleed, (SOB). The Unit was led by Major Baginski, SSGT Houser was SL (Squad Leader) that day, and I was, assigned TL (Team Leader). Like the rest of us, he was seeking shelter hunkered down, hidden in the edges of the jungle. Crouched under the broad leafs of the bush for protection against the unremitting rain. Our orders were to watch and report back to command anything of importance that came down the road. The enemy, NVA (North Vietnamese Army) and Charlie, the VC, (Vietcong), moved supplies with a substantial fighting force down the Ho Chí Minh Trail. All happening under the cover of violent rains in an attempt to conceal their activities; we often heard them; however, we could not see them. This day we were nine-miles into the northern mouth of the twenty-two mile stretch that led into A Shaw Valley, better known as The Valley of Death. Two high mountain ranges watched over the valley floor below on either side. No one knew it at the time, but this place would be the launching pad for the 1968 Tet Offensive.

I was twenty-two at the time, the military's laboring physical training had given me a body of iron; I was in the best shape of my life.

Trained in the art of infiltrating behind enemy lines, and for far more venomous purposes than just listening and reporting on what we observed moving on a trail, or crossing a dirt road on a mountainside.

It's been a little more than two-weeks since our last mission. With nothing to do but sit and wait for the rain to let up, my mind replays repeatedly what we had done just days before. We entered a small village near Hue; there were six of us then as well. Our team moved in under the cover of the jungle. Less than a klick later, we found a twelve-man Marine Recon Team, all dead. Finding them where they had been, ambushed. The bodies were rigged with booby-traps. We lost two of our original team members that day because of carelessness. While they were searching for the Marine's dog tags to call into command. Sergeant Korley, SL, (Squad Leader) tripped a Bouncing Betty. An explosive device that reaches two to four feet in height when triggered, killing Korley, exploding in all directions, spewing out glass, nails, and other nasty debris that also killed SSGT Wilson the Slack Man (Second Position) standing twenty-feet away.

This could not stand, we wanted revenge on the people who did this, and we were going to get it. Finding two VC in the nearby area overlooking the bodies, we captured and questioned them. We did what we did to get at the truth; they told us everything we needed to know. We wanted the people responsible for the massacre of the Marines and the deaths of our team members.

A Vietcong leader named, Binn, a name meaning 'peace' in Vietnamese had led the attack. He and his band were located just two-miles west of Plakue Vietnam. Near to where the 7/17 Air Cav. was located. We knew exactly where their village was.

Our immaturity, seem to guide us, at that age, we thought ourselves to be invincible. We were determined to seek out the evil men and punish for what they had done, believing all the while that we were doing the right thing. The following morning we had the two volunteer replacement team members we had requested, men who were already hardened to the task, at hand.

When the Huey arrived, I climbed in and sat by the open door. Removing my Ranger Issue Ka-Bar from its sheath, I began honing its edge with an oiled stone to insure it was ready for what was to come…

I never made it a practice of watching a man before striking him, even though they had taught us too. Based on my own experiences, I could always tell when someone had their eyes on me, and given enough time, I could spot him. I always gave the enemy the benefit of the doubt. Instead, I'd pick my targets out in turn, striking those in the outer most circles first as a rule, and then work my way in from there.

The techniques taught us by our instructors during hand-to-hand combat, had made us proficient at killing if nothing else. They taught us how to mentally accept and prepare for what we were, trained to do. So much so, that when it actually came to the physical duty of taking a life, it meant nothing more than a mere training exercise.

They taught us to be like the Apache Warriors of the Old West. Sure-footed and perfectly silent while stalking our prey, quietly coming in from behind the enemy and out of his line of vision, holding our breath so as not to be, heard. Then as quick as a rattlesnake, strike by interlocking an elbow up under his chin and across his throat. Followed by thrusting the blade through the ribs severing the spinal cord and entering the heart a fraction of a second later, holding him tight while he struggled to free himself. However unlike the Apache, there would no victory yell telling our teammates that a kill had been, made. Instead, I observed as the body as it slowly went limp in my arms, his spirit gradually draining from his dying carcass. Once I felt the final beat of his heart, and the ultimate release of his last breath of air. I took care in lowering his body to the ground as quietly as possible, watching his blood as it intermixed with the pooling rainwater.

If time permitted, I often left the SOB signature behind. They called us, 'Các suong mù ke giet nguoi' (The Fog Killers). Instead of a Death Card, we often pinned their right hand over their heart with their own knife. It scared the hell out of them.

Deed done, as the Apache I used the stealthiness of light and darkness together with the shadows I had appeared, rejoining my teammates at a predetermined point. Teammates who had returned from doing the same terrible things, with forty-three Viecong dead, and without a shot or a sound to disturb the quietness of the night, and satisfied with the results. We were, headed back to our own safe haven. Back to our own secure hovel, or at least, we prayed it to be so...

*President John F. Kennedy tells
the Nation that Cuba Has Missiles
10/22/1962*

CHAPTER TWO

THE INDUCTION 1962: My name is Jack Logan. My cousin Joseph Sacks, a red haired freckled faced kid from Kentucky got a wild hair the day we turned eighteen and decided to join the U.S. Army. After a battery of aptitude tests, which both of us were fortunate enough to score in the low nineties, on the mechanical portion of the exam? We were told us that they would send us to Fort Sill Oklahoma for our AIT (Advanced Individual Training) as mechanics for the military. With the condition, that first we had to complete the standard eight-week basic training course at Fort Gordon Georgia.

It was then I decided to keep a journal of events, of our experiences in the military. A diary if you will? Listing notable news events of the times as we went along, just seemed like the thing to do, something to look back on some day, so I did.

Our very first encounter of working with anything mechanical, or otherwise had come when they sent me to my grandparent's farm in 1958. My Cousin Joseph had preceded my arrival by three months. They had three-Ford tractors on the farm along with an old 1936 Ford pickup which they used to haul pigs to market. The farm was nestled in a valley of the Great Smokey Mountain's in North Carolina, not too far from Asheville and just west of Fontana Dam near the Cherokee Indian Reservation. The sprawling farmland consisted of more than seven-hundred acres, which sat at the southern base of Brown Mountain. My grandparents had used every square inch of it for farming. Our Uncle John Sacks had shown my Cousin Joseph and me the way around a toolbox, we were fourteen at the time.

As many before us, we arrived at Fort Gordon Georgia for our basic training. There were two-hundred of us in training; we were, divided into thirty-man-units and assigned to barracks where we lived, we had an array of Drill Instructors (DI's) who lorded over us. The primary duties of DI's were to break our wills, take away our individuality, emptying our young minds leaving nothing behind except a large chunk of clay. A chunk of clay awaiting the Master Sculptor's hand that began reshaping the clay, thereby reforming it into an image the military would be proud.

Our Master Sculptor had a name, Sergeant Carl J Beatty hailing from Bloomington Mississippi. He was a DI, and like his peers, he put forth his hands and began his dutiful task. His first step began by teaching us to have respect for others foremost, then ourselves, followed up with a good helping of personal responsibility.

Our work was to be, done with pride for teammates and ourselves. Secondly was responsibility to family, flag, and country. All the while constructing and ingraining into us only the highest standards of military discipline. The DI wanted what the US Army wanted, a well-sharpened military tool, a United States Army Soldier.

They had no way of knowing it, but Cousin Joseph and I were ahead of this game by, leaps and bounds.

My father died after finally scrumming to years of alcohol abuse in June 1958 at the age of forty-five. Turning fourteen and no one in the foster system willing to take me, I was, taken to live with my grandparents, John and Lesley Sacks on my mother's side of the family.

I had no idea what I was getting into; my dad had never talked about the farm in a favorable light. I never fully understood why until I ended up there. The very day I arrived at the farm, what my father had tried relating to me slap me in the face like stepping on the wrong end of a yard rake. I had entered a modern day prison the warden was my grandfather. My Uncle John filled the capacity of cell guard. My grandmother held the position of disciplinarian. Her duties were the dotting of one's head with a wooden spoon as the need arose. I often spent time in the old barn crying and counting the knots on my pumpkin' as Grandma Lesley had nicknamed my head.

The military had nothing on my grandfather. The man was seventy-four years old and lived only to whip that ass! In fact, for the first three months on the farm, my ass glowed in the dark. Learning to say yes sir and no sir and yes ma'am and no ma'am was the first order of business.

Working twelve to fifteen hours a day, provided little time to get in trouble. The farm was a dairy farm, a tobacco farm, a chicken farm, an egg farm, a cornfield farm, a vegetable farm, a pig farm; hell, my Uncle John even had an ant farm, you name it, they farmed it.

My cousin Joseph Sacks arrived at the farm by way of his mother, Faye. Uncle James Sacks, Joseph's dad had run off with another woman to God only knows where. Aunt Faye, growing restless and tired of being, strapped down by a kid she no longer wanted. She dumped Joseph off at the farm with no more regard than a sack of grain. She just drove up one bright morning, took Joseph out of the front seat, and his bag of belongings out of the backseat, sat both of them on the side porch of the white framed old house, then simply drove away. My grandmother hearing a child crying went out to investigate finding Cousin Joseph sitting on the porch steps. Looking like a dog-eared puppy that had just been, dropped off at the pound.

I on the other hand arrived by way of a Greyhound Bus; Uncle John met me at the bus station in town and drove me out to the farm.

Summertime had arrived, school was out which meant that school vacation was here. Fishing, swimming, horseback riding, hikes in the woods, drive in movies, everything fun was just waiting to happen. However, for two new farm boys with no real jobs, summertime meant more daylight and warmer temperatures to do more farm work. Everyone, including our young asses had to earn their keep; we learned there are no free rides in life. If we ate we worked, if we wanted a place to sleep, we paid.

We shared a single six by eight-foot bedroom, made from an unused attic space on the third floor of the old farmhouse. The transition had been completed by way of a couple of cobblers who called themselves carpenters, these guys could not spell carpenter, much less do the work of a skilled woodworker. We were paid two-dollars a day for seven days. We paid seven-dollars a week for food and found. We had to be up at three-thirty in the morning. Allowing us just enough time to brush our teeth, comb our hair, get dressed and report to the milk house at four, o'clock sharp each and every morning. If we were late, we were docked fifty-cent. God forbid if we were sick, because we were not, paid for the days that we didn't work regardless of the reason. They held us responsible for the seven-dollars a week for food and found. *'How are you going to learn responsibility if you don't know what responsibility is?'* Grandpas' voice often echoed in our heads. *'You must be at work on time and give your boss an honest day's work for an, honest day's pay if you want to keep your job.'*

In the milk house, there were a little more than three-hundred head of cattle averaging four nipples each just brimming with milk awaiting extraction. Still before, we could milk the cows. We had to treat the, utters with a chemical solution killing any bacteria. Once those chores were completed, we attached the suction cups.

Uncle John was a tall lean lanky man with dark green eyes, his face appearing as though it was always in need of a shave. A plaid colored checkered shirt accompanied by a pair of Levi's bib denim overalls, adorned his thin frame, and of course a grass green billed John Deere hat topped off his costume. However, the plaid shirt did change colors from time to time, other than that; his appearance remained pretty much the same. His top pocket often as not was, stuffed with a plug of mint chewing tobacco. Chomping on a corner plug and spitting wherever he pleased came standard with his harsh personality.

At one point or another in our lives, we have all heard the ole axiom '*He says what he means, and he means what he says*'. My Uncle John was the epitome of that saying. He explained things only once, if you forgot what he had said, or made the mistake of asking him to explain it again. He would knock you down and make you get up just so he could knock you down again. He did this until you fully understood what he had so carefully explained the first time around. If they had taught public schools in this manner, we would have a country overflowing with, geniuses'.

We finished with the milking around six a.m. every morning. Breakfast to follow; however before we could eat the morning meal, we had to clean the milk lines from where the suction cups attached to the cows. As well as the receiving lines and receiving tank, then we changed the filters responsible for filtering the milk, and then we had to shovel the fresh cow shit and wheel-bar it outside where we dumped it onto corrugated tin under the hot sun. After, drying for a week or, so it was, used for fertilizer.

Returning to the milk house, we cleaned the cement floors making it ready for the afternoon milking. Then around six-forty-five or so, once we washed our hands and went to the breakfast table with cow shit clinging to the cuffs of our pants. Changing clothes' wasn't an option; we just cleaned it off in the grass as we made our way to the kitchen table. After breakfast, we went to the hen house.

The first thing I learned was that brown eggs came from brown chickens, and white eggs came from white chickens. On a normal day, we gathered some twenty-cartons of eggs, there were forty-eight eggs to a layer, stacked twelve layers deep. Washing fresh chicken manure off the eggs was a real treat. I have never gagged so much in all of in my entire short little life. Then after washing the eggs, we went inside the chicken houses, cleaned the chicken shit out of the cages, as well as off the floor while the eggs dried. Afterwards, we fed the chickens that were, locked within their tiny little cages.

The automatic feeders seldom worked because they rarely serviced them. They were in constant need of repair; however, the cost of the parts wasn't something Grandpa wanted to invest. He was a strong believer in thrift. *'Since we have strong backs and willing hands, we can do without the trivial things that make life a little easier.'* Oh, he invited you to disagree with him if you didn't mind picking yourself up off the floor, and doing without breakfast, supper or all three meals. You could disagree as often as you wanted. Joseph and I disagreed with him as much as we wanted to. However eventually we gave in. Truth was, we damned near starved to death and had to quit.

We ate dinner as they called it around noon each day. At home in Norfolk Virginia, we called it lunch. After dinner, we cleaned the barn where they housed a few horses in need of Vet care and a couple of cows getting ready to deliver. Care was, taken not to mix the cow's food with the horse's provisions; such a mistake could kill a horse. We fed the horses hay from the upper lofts, poured grain into the feeding troughs, and of course picked up more shit. Around two in the afternoon, we gassed up the tractors, checked the oil. Then we cleaned the dry earth from the blades of the plows, making them ready for the night's plowing.

Then we returned to the milk house around a quarter-to-four in the afternoon, where we began our milking session anew. Finishing around six-thirty in the evening, we ate supper, then reported to the tractors, and headed for the fields. My grandfather believed in the Bible, somewhere in there it said to *'Let the Land rest once every seven years;'* My Grandpa John's idea of letting the land rest was to plow it to death. He wanted the resting land plowed, and disked until the soil was so fine it slipped through your fingers like sand. We would have done more plowing, but Grandpa confessed saying, *'Even we needed some sleep once and awhile'.* So around ten-thirty every night we would turn the tractor's toward home letting the pale headlights guided our way. *'Besides, there is always tomorrow night unless it rains'.* He told us. Joseph and I prayed for rain every night of the week before going to bed, even so, the rain never came.

The work on the farm was seven days a week, three-hundred and sixty-five days a year, year after year.

There for a while I believed that I had been a bad person in another life, and the farm was my personal hell to endure for eternity. There was no electric lighting, no plumbing, and only one outhouse for six people. Traveling sixty-feet at four in the morning in twenty-degree weather for a relieving pee was bad enough, yet finding the damn thing occupied was a real heartbreaker.

Time they say cures all ills, and our time had finally come. Joseph turned eighteen first, I followed two months later, and we left the farm at four a.m. on a Sunday morning never looking back. Each of us leaving our own hand written notes, right in the middle of the dining table in the kitchen where it could be easily, found: I was in somewhat of a hurry. I wrote mine in short order: *'Dear Grandpa and Grandma, thank you for the life lessons, your grandson, Jack'.*

Time had sat us free, time had become our friend, and I equated this day to being, released from prison. However, unlike prison, there wasn't anyone outside the front gate by the old road. Offering us a ride to town, therefore, we walked the whole six miles to the city, never regretting one-step of it. With one-hundred and seventy-one dollars between us, we rented a motel room for the night. The next morning, we ate in a sit-down restaurant for the second time in four years.

Early Monday morning the two of us walked, down to the army recruiting office in hope of enlisting into the US Army. We told the recruiter we were not waiting for the government to draft us, because our grandpa had told us just how slow those fools in Washington could be at times. No sir, we were not waiting, we wanted to join right then, and there. We enlisted for a full three years each, leaving out the fact that we were, related. The recruiter did suggest that we join on the buddy system, which meant that we would be together during Basic Training & AIT, (Advanced Individual Training). After AIT, we would be at the mercy of the military as to where they would send us.

I have to say that Basic Training was one of the best times of my life. I thought of it as an Advance Boy Scout Training Camp of sorts. We slept two hours longer in the morning not having to get up until five-thirty. Once up we reported for a head count, making sure no one had ran away in the middle of the night. Then we either went for a mile run or did in place exercising for thirty-minutes while working up an appetite for breakfast. It was great. In the mess hall, we could take as much food as we wanted as long as we ate what we took. Then we would go out to do some pretend hand-to-hand combat and then play some king of the hill with fugal sticks. Climb a few poles, and shoot a few guns, we were just a bunch of kids having fun. Once, we had to crawl through some mud-filled trenches with poles on either side of us. Barbed wire overhead in an attempt at simulating real war, then this fool in a machine-gun nest began firing live rounds over our heads screaming, *'Keep your goddamn head's down!'* What did he think we were going to do, standup? After ducking bullets, we ate lunch around noon, and then went back out, shooting more guns or attend more boring classes about catching the clap.

One day we had to report for roll call in the middle of the day during our third week of training. It seemed two of the guys decided to go Absent Without Leave. (AWOL) They had simply walked away shortly after afternoon chow. With no cow shit, horseshit, pig shit, chicken shit, dog shit, or cat shit to pickup, that plus the fact, we were having the best times of our lives. Joseph and I could not figure out why anyone would deliberately leave the fort. Later, we heard that they had been, arrested by the military police.

If I had known where they, were being held. I would have offered their superiors my grandparent's address.

This one day, I gave some serious thought of going AWOL myself. We were standing in formation as ordered. Then told that they were taking us to the gas chamber, I have to be honest; this scared the living crap out of me. My Dad had told me only bad people like Julius and Ethel Rosenberg. Who had been, found guilty of spying against America were sent to the gas chamber for their crimes. I could understand it happening to someone like those two, but none of us was spies. So why were we being sent to the gas chamber? I didn't get it.

Drill Sergeant Beatty tried his best to ease my fears, "You stupid unintelligent piece of fuckin' road kill! What the fuck is wrong with you!"

I think he was trying to tell me something.

"The Rosenberg's went to the electric chair and not the gas chamber numb nuts!" Then with a gleam in his eye, he put his hand on my shoulder and a wide smile expressed, "I am so sorry that Fort Gordon doesn't have an electric chair! I would love to strap your bony ass in it and show you the difference. Light you up! See if your eyeballs rotate!"

He always had our best interest at heart, and a great way of making a person feel better about themselves.

At first, the gas chamber wasn't that bad; they taught us how to put on our masks properly and how to check it for leaks. Then came the gas pellets, they dropped them into one of the metal cans while we stood there waiting for the room to fill with vapors.

Sergeant Beatty walking up to me, "Do you smell anything, soldier?"

No, indicating by shaking my head, I wasn't about to take the mask off just to answer him.

Jerking the mask from my face, "What about now Dickhead!" Screaming at the top of his voice.

My eyes began swelling with tears as I breathed in the gas. "Yessir, now I do!"

"Don't call me sir you silly sonofabitch dumb ass piece of shit! I work for a living! My first name is on my sleeve and my last name is on my chest!"

"Yes Sergeant."

"Now get the fuck outta my face!"

"Yes Sergeant!" Running out of the back door trying not to rub my eyes.

The part I liked about basic the best though was the group singing, which happened almost every time we went marching.

On the farm, the warden forced us to listen to Country Music all day. Johnny Cash, Carl Perkins, Kitty Wells, Dolly Parton, Buck Owens, and so forth, personally, I liked Duane Eddie, Bobby Darren, Elvis, Buddy Holly, Fats Domino, and others. However, we never listen to them until Grandpa finally gave in and had electricity installed to the old place. Joseph and I were saving our money so we could escape when the time came. We were too frugal to buy a portable radio that needed all of those batteries. However, now that we had electricity, we rushed out and purchased a cheap radio.

Yet, here at Fort Gordon we sang songs I had never heard of before. Songs like *'I don't know but I've been told people from Georgia have a rubber, asshole!'* In addition was, *'I've gotta a girl dressed in red! She makes a living on a feather bed!'* Another was, *'I don't know but I've been told Eskimo pussy's mighty cold!'* I didn't particularly care for that song, I felt it made fun of women, but Joseph liked it, he went around singing it all of the time.

We had made up a song about, Sergeant Carl Beatty, our primary Sadist for what he had done to us two-weeks earlier. Yet we had to wait until the right time to spring it on him. It happened this way. Sergeant Beatty, a black man from Bloomington Mississippi who had to be in his mid-forties at least, and twenty pounds overweight chewing on cigars like, they were going out of style. The cigar had become his personal signature. When you spotted Beatty he had a cigar either in his mouth or between his fingers, he was never without one.

"All right soldiers', we are going on a four-mile run this morning!" He said as seriously as it, could be said.

Murmuring to the others trying not to be, overheard, "Like this going to happen, this turkey won't make a half mile without dropping like a rock!"

In spite of everything, we began. We started double-timing with Beatty counting cadence, first, the left and then the right foot. "Hup! Tup! Thrup! Fourp!" On and on this went as the first mile continued, then came the second mile, he's still not showing any signs of getting tired. "Hup! Tup! Thrup! Fourp!" This guy cannot be for real I'm thinking, yet there he is pounding the ground still chirping, "Hup! Tup! Thrup! Fourp!"

Others began lagging behind a bit, which caught hell from the DI's bringing up the rear. I had begun getting tired too, but I wasn't about to quit. Joseph was three rows behind me when we started; even he had fallen back to sixth place. "What are you looking at turd face?" Beatty's creaming, "Eyes front!"

"Yes Sergeant," as I gasped for air.

"Hup! Tup! Thrup! Fourp!"

We were dying as we approached the end of the second mile. I believed we were all hoping he would just drop dead of a heart attack, at least I was thinking it.

"Column left! Hoe!"

We turned.

"Column left! Hoe!"

Turning again wondering why they just didn't have a command for a U-turn. *'U-turn Hoe!'* I mused. Now wouldn't a command such as that be much simpler? Yet, the pace never slacked, the sonofabitch cigar smoking overweight out of shape ground pounding fool was killing me! Still, there he is broadcasting his favorite words, "Hup! Tup! Thrup! Fourp!" This man is like a goddamn machine showing no signs of exhaustion, still breathing, still shouting his cadence, "Hup! Tup! Thrup! Fourp!" His cigar hanging out of the right side of his face.

Growing weaker with every step, but determined not to quit, I plowed along. Half way through the fourth-mile, I begin thinking about quitting. I had falling way behind; my legs were becoming overwhelmed with pain, my shin splints were screaming at me. It felt as though the muscles were literally coming off the bones.

"Hup! Tup! Thrup! Fourp!"

"Man, fuck this," I muttered.

"Listen Up people! The first five who make it with me to the end will not have to do Kitchen Police (KP) for the remainder of their basic training!"

That inspired my young ass, mainly because I hated mess hall detail, cleaning grease traps, mopping floors, cleaning tables, mopping floors and washing dishes was the pits. Therefore, I ignored the pain in my legs, and began stepping up the pace.

"Hup! Tup! Thrup! Fourp!"

I had worked my way into third-place; and it was all I could do to stay there. Reaching deep down within myself, I pulled every ounce of energy I had left in my body to the surface

I had committed myself to running faster and farther than anyone running against me with his, "Hup! Tup! Thrup! Fourp!" Barking in my ears.

Thank God! I crossed the finish line in third place! Once there, I hit the ground on my knees rolling over on my back rubbing my lower legs with both hands, massaging the right leg and the left one. God they hurt.

Then it came, "On your feet!"

The five of us shot to our feet as ordered, we watched as the slow pokes that were just finishing the run as they finally caught up with us.

To the five of us came, "You Meatheads! You are the worst group of recruits I have ever seen in my entire goddamn military career! My grandmother could do better! I do not recall anyone telling you Poster Children for Stupidity to run! This is a double-timed exercise event people! If you can't follow orders here, how are you going to follow orders on the field?"

Private Adams raised his hand.

"We are not in school private! Ask your goddamn question!"

"Yes Sergeant, do the first five still win?"

"Yes private, the first five still win! You get to run another mile with me!" Beatty added.

"But?"

"Your butt is three-inches away from your dick private! Now, fall in on me!"

Devastated, not to mention pissed, we realized all of what he had told us was nothing more than crap on his part. He wanted us to win only to chop us off at the knees as he had done at least twenty times before. You would think we would learn.

"Single column dickheads! Act like professional soldiers even if you aren't." Beatty scowled.

With no other options available to us, we fell in line and made ready.

"You are to keep this interval between you at all times. Extend your right arm out touching the right shoulder of the dickhead standing in front of you!"

We did.

"Now! Hup! Tup! Thrup! Fourp!"

The pain had returned to my legs almost immediately, still as before, I made a pledge to myself to keep up, just as before, he never let up until we had run the entire mile. We didn't run a half mile, turn around, and run back toward the base. No! We ran the whole mile, and then turned around marching back making it two miles collectively. During the moment of realizing, the full extent of what he had done to us, I made it my personal mission to make him pay for his sins.

Getting back to the song, we made up for Sergeant Beatty. It's the last week of training; and we were on a forced ten-mile march for nothing other than giving us something to do. I didn't complain, didn't matter what we did, at least it didn't involve picking up shit anymore, or milking cows or doing God's work plowing field for half the night. Marching was just fine with me, personally. I didn't care how I spent the days, anything is better than spending them on the farm. Besides, we were off at five almost every day. We went to bed at ten every night with Taps playing a lullaby in the distance. So what was there to complain about? Anyway, after covering four-miles of the ten-mile march, Sergeant Beatty let us take a short break, we had stopped at a stand of large Pine trees along by a well-worn path made by our predecessors, we were allowed to drink from our canteens and smoke if we had'em. Sergeant Beatty removed the cap from his canteen, took a long swallow. Then immediately steps back and began spewing the mouth full of fluid all over the ground and a couple of people standing too close to him. He even spit out his cigar, which had been a first for me He began coughing and hacking violently.

Catching his breath, "Who the hell, pissed in my canteen?" He yelled at the top of his voice...

The whole column broke out with laughter; I for one would never tell who had done it to him, besides his reaction to it had been funny as hell. During the last few days of basic training, we were, allowed too as Squad Leader, call out our own cadence and sing our own songs.

This kid, Scott Haven from South Dakota was acting Squad Leader on the day, we sang our song, "Hut! Two! Three! Four!" Scott yelled as we marched to his beat. "Okay soldiers, we have a new song today, so keep up!"

"We will," we, shot back.

"Hut! Two! Three! Four! Sergeant Beatty's turning green!"

We followed with the chorus, "Sergeant Beatty's turning green!"

"Somebody pissed in his canteen!"

Again, in unison we followed with. "Somebody pissed in his canteen!"

Sergeant Beatty was on us like a pounding rainstorm, going straight for poor ole Scott. "You pissed in my canteen didn't you, you fuckin' maggot? Tell me the truth! Was it you?"

Scotts' about to cry, "No Sergeant, Private Logan did it Drill Sergeant!"

Well, the jig was up. Since I am the only Private Logan in the outfit, I had this sinking feeling that he knew exactly where to find me. He came for me like a barn fly drawn to horseshit!

"Well funny man! What do you have to say for yourself?" His lit cigar only an inch from my face, with my eyes watering from the stinging smoke, "I think I am going to fail your dumb ass just so I can keep you here with me for another eight weeks Private!"

"I would like that, Sergeant! I like you a lot. And I really don't have anything else planned for the rest of the summer!"

Laughter sprang out.

"Assume the position asshole!" His face expressing his anger, "Give me one-hundred pushups!" Pointing to the ground with the cigar in hand.

"Yes Sergeant!" I dropped and began cranking them out.

"Everyone else, drop! I want hundred just like your friend Private Logan," he growled. "In addition, while you are down there, you can thank him for this opportunity to serve me!"

After the ordeal was over, a few of the guys bitched at me for what I had done; still, most of them thought it was funny.

Later in the afternoon, I went to Sergeant. Beatty's quarters and asked to speak with him. He came out of his barracks as his usual charming self. Frowning, "What the fuck do you want, ass wipe?" As always sucking on his cigar.

I stood at attention, "Permission to speak freely Sergeant?"

"At ease maggot, say whatever it is you have on your puny little mind, and then get the fuck out of my face!"

"Sergeant Beatty, I would like to apologize to you for what I did. I have no excuse for my actions."

"Fuck off! Piss Ant!" Standing there like a rock.

"I just wanted to apologize for my actions," gesturing with my hands.

"Well I am not in a forgiving fucking mood, try catching me tomorrow!" Then he simply turned and walked back into his quarters leaving me there.

We are not about to send American boys
nine or ten thousand miles away from home
to do what Asian boys ought to be doing
for themselves.
Lyndon Johnson

CHAPTER THREE

AIT AND BEYOND: After Basic, I wrote to Sergeant Beatty not knowing if he would write back.

From Fort Gordon, they sent Joseph and me to Fort Sill Oklahoma as promised for our AIT. Sixteen-weeks later, we graduated with a Wheel Vehicle Maintenance Degree in hand. It was then we received orders regarding our new duty assignments.

Joseph was on his way to Fort Hood Texas where he had been, assigned to the 32nd Armor Division.

I went to Fort Lewis Washington where I was, placed with A Battery 32nd Artillery, just a few miles from Seattle.

Working at the motor pool maintenance shack for just two short months, they promoted me to Private First

Class. I enjoyed the work yet the officer's in charge had no idea which way was up. I just gave the *yes sir's* they wanted and went about my business. After three months of yessir I received another stripe, as a Specialist E-4, my pay increased to eighty-nine dollars a month, I was on my way up!

Joseph always called me the first of every month; neither of us was any good at writing letters, so we didn't. During his last phone call, he told me that an officer had told him the military was running short on helicopter mechanics, explaining that I should check it out. I had expressed the fact that I would like to work on airplanes when I got out of the service. Only because aircraft mechanics made a lot of money in civilian life, so he had called to give me a heads up. Therefore, after giving it some thought, I put in a request for a MOS change. The request went through, and sixty-days later, I reported to Fort Eustis Virginia for a twenty-six Rotary Wing Training course, just twenty-miles away from my old stomping grounds in Norfolk VA. They changed my MOS from level one too critical. Critical meaning they didn't have enough people to fill that position, which meant being, approved for a different MOS could be difficult, if not impossible.

Graduating in the top eighty-percent of the class, I received orders to report to the 568th Transportation Company in Fairbanks Alaska, namely Fort Wainwright. At sixty-below, working up a sweat would be the least of my worries.

While stationed in Alaska, I found myself as far away from Joseph and Texas as I could possibly be. After four months at Fort Wainwright, I received a promotion to Specialist E-5, which got me forty-two more dollars a month. Now I could afford to send my laundry out instead of doing it myself.

I missed some of the people I had met at Fort Lewis. However, it seemed the acquaintances in the military never seem to stick. Oh, we exchanged addresses and promises to write ok, but somehow we just never got around to it.

It was Christmas Eve; I had been expecting a package from my grandparents. They had been great about sending cookies with only the best of pies on the planet for birthdays and holidays to both Joseph and me.

Checking the mail, I received one small package from them filled with all different kinds of cookies. To my surprise, I had also received an overly stuffed envelope from Mary Beatty. Believing it to be a Christmas card, I stuffed it in my coat pocket intending to read it later. A group of us went for evening chow before returning to the barracks for the night. Its fifty-eight degrees-below, that and having, been blessed with seven feet of accumulated snow over the last six days. It made it almost impossible to go to town or anywhere else for that matter. Later we went about exchanging gifts and wishing each other a Merry Christmas.

The Guns of Darkness with David Niven had just begun on channel 5 and I wanted to watch it. I had forgotten all about the Christmas card until I took my jacket off and found it. With my roommate Specialist Millen being away on a thirty-day leave back in Maryland, I locked the door and settled down on the bed to enjoy the movie and read the card. Opening the envelope, I realized it wasn't a card at all, but rather a hand written letter. I assumed that Mary Beatty was Sergeant Beatty's wife. However, as it turned out, Mary Beatty was the Sergeant' smother. The letter had a couple of military forms in with it.

Dear Mr. Logan,

I hope this letter finds you well. It is with a burdened heart I tell you this. Our son Carl Beatty died almost three months ago to the day. Carl had a heart attack and died on the parade field of his beloved Fort Gordon.

The army has forwarded his personal affects to us. Your letter to him was, found among those papers. I do not know if he responded to your letter or not. In any case, I thought I would answer.

I also thought you might like reading what military notes he had since you are in the service yourself. You may keep them if you like we have copies.

He loved his country and fought for our freedom, as you yourself may have to do one day. He was in Korea as an Army Ranger in the 1950's. I believe he was 39 when they sent him there. My husband and I were his family, but the Army has always been his life.

Something happened to him in Korea during the period he was there. All he ever said about it

*to us was that he hated himself for being a Negro.
Because of his race, his Ranger team was, disbanded
near the end of the conflict.*

Sincerely, Mary Beatty

Tears came to my eyes as I picked up the first form,
it read: *'The Rangers Creed.'* I thought it a bit hokey until
read line A, the second letter in the Ranger Creed.

*'Acknowledging the fact that a Ranger is a more elite
soldier who arrives at the cutting edge of battle by land, sea, or
air, I accept the fact that as a Ranger my country expects me to
move further, faster, and fight harder than any other soldier.'*

Almost to the point of sobbing, my mind went back
to the four-mile jogging incident during basic training;
he had never been out of breath or seemed to get tired.

Wiping a tear and looking over another of the forms I
came across a copy of military records with a good portion
of it blacked out, while the rest of it was blurred, and hard
to read. Then I found a small card about the size of a social
security card, it had the word, Ranger printed in the center
of it. A telephone number, with the names Mom and Dad
circled in the upper left corner. I put the card in my wallet
promising myself I would call the number one day.

Once I finished my eight months in Alaska and by sheer
luck, they shipped me to Texas and to Joseph. Fort Hood
remained his only duty station throughout his enlistment.

Reaching Fort Hood, I took the bus to my new billets
at the1st Calvary Company housed near the airport.
I liked my new duty assignment. They promoted me

from Specialist Fifth Class to Sergeant E6 for a purpose. They put me in charge of the maintenance section in an attempt to get me to stay in the army. The extra stripe had brought the highest pay raise thus far.

Spending time at Fort Gordon, Fort Sill Oklahoma, Fort Lewis Washington, Fort Eustis Virginia, and Fort Wainwright Alaska had pretty much eaten up the three-year enlistment. At this point, I had ninety-days and a wake up until my three years of duty to my country was over. I wanted to stay in the military, but not as an aircraft mechanic.

For the next two-months, I went to work every day thinking of Sergeant Beatty and the Army Rangers, the more I found out about the Rangers. The more interested and impressed I had become. I talked to Joseph about what I had learned of Sergeant Beatty and the Rangers.

As it turned out, Joseph decided to go with me to the on post recruiter and pick up some brochures on the subject.

The recruiter explained to us that the training would be far different then what we endured during the basic training at Fort Gordon. He didn't expound on his statement other than to say. That out of every one-hundred men who had joined the Ranger school, only thirty-percent of them actually made it through the program on average. Regardless, after a few more weeks of researching, Joseph and I decided to apply.

After a few written tests and another series of aptitude tests, a physical exam, and something new, a series of physiological tests, we were, instructed to wait to hear from admissions.

On 03 June 1965, we enlisted for another, three-years and was, accepted into the Rangers' training camp. We received orders to report to Fort Binning Georgia on 20 June 1965.

They told us that we were, handpicked for extending training while there. Furthermore, we would go to Fort Riley Kansas for additional training if we graduated the course. No further explanation was, given.

I can tell you the sixty-nine days of training, was nothing even remotely like the basic training we had experienced back in Georgia? Firstly, we were, stripped of our ranks. Every man started as an equal officer and enlisted alike. They didn't want us favoring one individual over another. What they did want were men who worked to achieve the same objectives and goals as a collective team. When tasked to do so, we had to complete the mission as an individual in case a Ranger ended up the lone survivor.

The hand-to-hand combat was not the protective padded ends of the pugil stick as it had been at Fort Gordon, where we knocked each other off a platform while playing king of the hill.

We learned that the Apache Indians were America's first guerilla fighting force. Their hand-to-hand combat skills put fear into every enemy of the Apache. The word *Apache* comes from the *Yuma* word for (Fighting-Men). It also comes from a *Zuni* word meaning (Fighting the *Enemy*). Over the years, the military slowly adopted the Killing Skills of the Apache as their own. U.S. Army Rangers hand-to-hand combat is in part, based on the Apache's basic techniques. Adding Martial Arts took the Apache's methods of fighting to sheer perfection.

The training taught each of us how to kill quickly and quietly in three seconds or less should the need arise. Although there were many techniques, moves and terms, it all boiled down to, Engage, Terminate, and Move On.

Farther training included day and night land navigation. Daily physical training, map reading, airborne operations, Ranger standards, five-mile runs which had to be completed in less than eight minutes per mile. Facing combative forces in the field and at their posts, combat water survival test, six, eight and ten mile road marches, driver training, fast rope training, combat lifesaving with certification and on it went.

The song's we had sang for fun back at Fort Gordon, had taken a more sinister turn.

I wanna be an Airborne Ranger,
I wanna live a life of danger,
I wanna go to Vietnam,
I wanna kill the Viecong.

I learned first-hand what the recruiter meant when he said that only thirty-percent of recruits on the average would make it here. We lost forty-one people in just two short weeks.

Months before our training ever started, America had already taken the first step of committing itself to war against Vietnam. Washington accused North Vietnam of attacking the USS Turner Joy and the USS Maddox with gunboats in The Gulf of Tonkin. Based on those allegations and others, President Lyndon Baines Johnson requested the United States Congress to pass the Gulf of Tonkin Resolution as soon as possible. This document gave President Johnson the authority '*to take all necessary measures to repel any armed attack against the forces of the United States and to prevent any further aggression. With the approval of the of Tonkin Resolution*' Johnson ordered the intense bombing of North Vietnam, and on 7 February 1965, B-52's, from the Air Force did just that. Regular bombing runs began over North Vietnam's populated areas striking military targets. At nearly the same time, Johnson promised more troops for the support forth South Vietnamese Army, and our ground forces already in South Vietnam as advisors.

'*On 9 February 1965, US Marines are, ordered to Vietnam, and on 8 March 1965, 3,500 arrived on Asian soil, appearing more and more that the US was in for the long haul*', UPI Radio.

Our drill instructors told us clearly that our going to Vietnam was unquestionable; they advised us to learn the Vietnamese language and their culture, instructing us to learn it well. '*You cannot fight your enemy, unless you know your enemy inside and out.*'

Ninety-days later, and completing the added unique education, we were finally at the end of this stage of our training. Two days later, twenty-eight of us were on a plane heading to Fort Riley Kansas. For reasons neither of us knew, we were forbidden to discuss the training we were about to undergo. Once this training was completed, and four-weeks later, a hand full of us ended up with no permanent assignment.

They told what was left of our group to stand down until further notice. A month later, we were, told that an assignment would come after reaching Vietnam.

Then at last, we were on our way, going by way of the USS Gordon. Joseph thought the name of the ship would be our good luck charm since we had gone through basic training at an army fort with the same name, Gordon. Of course, he had milked cows for a living, what, the hell did he know?

By ship, it took us twenty-one days to reach Vietnam. All I did the whole time was eat, study Vietnamese, and throw up every hour on the hour. They told me there were over three thousand men aboard the, Gordon. During those twenty-one days, I managed to meet three of them; we had said '*Hi*' to each other while we were hanging over the guardrail puking.

Once we arrived in Vietnam, I got off the ship and kissed the sand. Of course, it's raining which caused me to laugh at my luck. My mind returning to those nights of endless plowing in those dusty fields on the farm, and the rain we had prayed for that never came.

It's beautiful here despite the rain, the swaying palm trees, the beaches, the lush green valleys, and hillsides. I marveled at the almost perfect engineering on earth, the rice paddies, and as Joseph kept repeating, *'the women!'* The roads were mostly dirt although near the larger cities. Some were, paved by the French years ago. The Army Corps of Engineers maintained the road system at present.

I had never seen so much green in my life. Our instructors had told us during our survival training while walking through the swamps back home, that our swamps and under growth had nothing on the jungles of Vietnam. We had mock ups' of hooch's and had been presented with war situations to gain a feel for the real thing, understanding that the real thing would be considerably different from anything encountered back home.

The military wasted no time in building and installing small supply bases throughout South Vietnam. Da Nang, in the North Country for one reason or another grew the fastest; it sprang up almost seemly overnight, growing from a few warehouses to hundreds. Resulting in acres upon acres of buildings and supply yards. Cam Ranh Bay, which is located on the shores of The South China Sea in II Corps, had become one of the largest seaports in the world. The Army Republic of South Vietnam soldiers stationed there; the very army we had come to help in the fight against communism.

However, Long Binh was by far the largest land base port; Long Binh housed mostly Military Police, LBJ's Camp and stockade as well as other indigenous personal. Located just north of Saigon, the base was the main entry point to Asian soil, it was the replacement center for almost anything Army, and it was only a matter of time before the base would be, packed to its limit. At the same time on 28 July 1965, President Johnson had increased the count of US troops in South Vietnam from 75,000 to 125,000 as reported by UPI Radio…

Our purpose in Vietnam is to prevent the
Success of aggression. It is not a
conquest, it is not empire, it is not foreign
bases, it is not domination. It is, simply put,
just to prevent the forceful conquest
of South Vietnam by North Vietnam.
Lyndon B. Johnson

CHAPTER FOUR

OUR NEW HOME: Upon arriving in Vietnam, Joseph and I were stuck in a limbo state, not having a company as such to report. We were assigned to a two-bedroom apartment with two single beds in each. All of the furnishings were military style furniture. I mention this only because they all looked alike. At night when we returned from our all night drinking sessions, as often as not, ended up trying to enter the wrong apartment. The stunt often got us screamed at and sometimes even threatened. The Military Police stationed there were responsible for patrolling and guarding every security point throughout the base. These people worked in eight-hour shifts twenty-four hours a day seven days a week; they didn't care much for interruptions while they were sleeping.

Four of was delegated to the apartment. We had no idea if there were more like us waiting to be, assigned or not. Joseph and I moved into the front bedroom overlooking the street below. SGT. Andy Layton, one of the men I remembered meeting for the first time while hanging over the rail on the USS Gordon. SSG> Sims was the fourth man, he too was on the Gordon, but I never met him until today.

We were to live with the military police as ordered to await farther instructions. The complex was just off Bien Shau Street inside the main post at Long Binh. The apartment complexes were a huge sixteen building complex standing three-story's high with four apartments per level, sixteen apartments per building.

SGT. Layton was a stocky man, yet, not fat by any means. He stands five-eight a tempered frame of pure muscle. Harden by working the rigs of the Louisiana oil fields. Two years into the job, his dad died, shortly after that Layton joined the army, leaving his mother and a sister behind.

Jimmy Sims, a thin man spoke with a slight stutter when he got nervous. His dark hair, and eyes accompanied by a square chin, reminded me of those shifty-eyed gangsters I had seen in all of the Al Capone movies. That and the fact that he was from Chicago, seemed to confirm it. He always quiet when he wasn't walking around passing gas; he kept pretty much to himself. We would see him on occasion at night dressed in only his dark green boxers, pacing back and forth between the kitchen and his bathroom. It was rare, but at times, he opened up a bit, still, he never talked about himself. Sims bunked with SGT. Layton who often slept on the sofa, reporting that SGT. Sims smelled like shit.

Then on a Saturday morning almost a month later, a Lieutenant Ramsey called us from Joint Special Operations Command. (JSOC) He's coming over at 0900 ZULU Sunday morning to talk with us about earning our keep as Rangers.

Since, we didn't have anything else planned for Sunday, we agreed as if we had a choice in the matter.

* * * *

SGT Layton answered the knock at the door; we were dressed in our standard olive drab fatigues with polished boots that you could see your face, the four of us standing by the door.

Layton opened it, "Come in Lieutenant, please," Layton, responded holding to the doorknob.

"Thank you Gentlemen," Lt. Ramsey said as he walked in removing his hat.

Layton moving closer, "Sir would you like something to drink?"

Lt. Ramsey loosening his collar, "You, guys got any beer?"

"Yes Sir," Layton left to fill the order.

Lt. Ramsey motioned to the chairs and sofa, "Let's sit, Gentlemen."

Layton returned handing Ramsey a bottle of Pabst Blue Ribbon Beer taking a chair across from him.

"Gentlemen, we lost track of you, Major Baginski had wanted to speak to each of you in person, but he's been called to Washington," he sighed. "To be honest you guys fell through the cracks," he smiled. "The Major will not be back for another two-week, at this point, we are stuck as to what to do with you?"

Joseph is the first to speak up. "We're up for just about anything sir; we're tired of just sitting around doing nothing."

"So what about chow and laundry, are you all right in those areas?"

"Yessir," I said. "We eat chow with the Military Police; we also have a washer and dryer in house."

He looked around, "Good, good," removing a folded piece of paper from his pocket. "There is an area north of here, a declared safe area. As quad of Marines is up there as we speak on a mop up operation. What we need is a Ranger Long Range Reconnaissance Patrol (LRRP) go up there, Recon the area east of their position. It would give you men some practical field experience."

"Sounds good, Sir," Layton spoke up.

"Do either of you have combat experience?"

"No Sir, we don't," I confessed.

"It doesn't matter. Like, I said, the area is a safe area. It will just provide you people with something to do while we are waiting on the Major's return."

"Yessir."

"You will need your full gear, everything in your rucksack, explosives, det cords, claymores, and grenades, munitions along with all of which can be obtained through supply here on the base. What you carry for food is up to you of course."

"Yessir."

"Here is an order of reacquisition; they will let you have what you need. One field radio should be sufficient," speaking as if he were tired and wanted to lie down.

"Yessir."

"A 2 ½ ton will be by early tomorrow morning to pick you up. Be at gate at 0400, from there the driver will take you to the airfield. At the airfield, you will, be taken by Huey to Tay Ninh Province, forty-two miles east of the Cambodian border in III Corps. Another small Ranger team will meet you there; SGT. Charles Blevins will be Team Leader for both teams. His team consists of three members; however, your instructions are to work as one collective team. Is that clear?"

"Yessir," I answered with the others.

You can kill ten of my men for everyone I kill of yours, but even at those odds, you will lose and I will win.
Ho Chí Minh
Vietnamese pronunciation: Hô⬜ T⬜ĭm⬜⬜.
Born, Nguyen Sinh Cung, also known
as Nguyen Ái Quoc
1890 ~ 1969

CHAPTER FIVE

BREAKING OUR CHERRY: It was raining just as it had all night, an oddity for November, which is supposed to be a dry month. The Weather Man promised the rain is part of a small system passing through which should end by early morning. As Lt. Ramsey promised we were, picked up at the gate and taken to the airfield.

As, Rangers we were provided a variety of small arms we carried into the field. The two preferred weapons were the M-60 light machinegun along with the M-16. They had modified both weapons for our use in the field; some had collapsible stocks made of lightweight plastic grips, anything to reduce their weight. They modified the M-60 machine-gun nicknamed the *'Pig'*. By, replacing the heavy metal parts with lighter metals, and removing the nonessential metal parts altogether. They also replaced the solid stocks with helicopter gunner plastic stocks. It made the M-60 light enough to be, fired from the hip if necessary. Although primarily the changes were, made so that it could, be carried one-handed for long distances without stopping to rest as often.

We also had access to the SKS and the AK-47 assault rifles depending on mission tasks. The M-14 was, replaced by the M-16, the M-14 had a 7.62 mm round, which were heavier than the M-16, and theM-16 had a selectable lever for full and semi or automatic fire. The M16 was to have had the same effective range as the M-14 rifle it replaced, but it was most effective at a range of 215 yards (200m) or less. The M16 used a 5.56mm (.223 cal.) cartridge in 20- or 30-round magazines, which weighed less so we could carry more ammunition. The Swedish made K-9mm submachine-gun was my weapon of choice; they suppressed the K-9 to reduce the noise as they had some other weapons. It sounded like someone spitting when fired, making it undetectable at twenty-yards.

Today, everyone except me carried the M-16. I had the K-9 over my shoulder with the barrel pointing down in an attempt to keep it out the rain. Once we stepped down out of the truck, we made our way to the Huey UH1B Helicopter sitting on the landing pad with its clearance lights flashing, its TL-53 jet engine idling like a monster waiting to, be released. Coming into the pilot's view, he began increasing the RPM's, the sound of the centrifugal clutch engaging was unmistakable, the rotating blades slowly increasing with each spin of the blade. Atop the rotor mast, holding the rotor blades in place was a single flat nut with a locking washer. This was called a Jesus Nut, and aptly so, if somehow the Jesus Nut got damaged and broke off, Jesus Himself was all that you had between you and the ground.

Opening the sliding door, we stepped up into the craft, the first thing; we saw were the flak jackets lying on top of the seats. We picked a seat; and not knowing any better, each of us in turn tossed the flak jackets onto the floor.

The door gunner, a short man wearing a flight helmet leaned into to us. "You want to sit on those flak jackets!" Screaming over the noise of the chopper pointing at the vest, "They help keep you from being shot in the ass! I suggest you sit on them if you don't want to die!"

Apprehension began to sit in, each of us fearing what may or may not happen or exactly what to expect next. Our faces reflected the fear as we placed the flak jackets back onto the seats and sat down.

In a matter of seconds, we were airborne. The pilot had the chopper heading northwest into the breaking sunrise off in the distance; the clouds were thinning a bit as the sun peaked through.

The pounding, of the wipers seem to match the beat of the popping blades as they cut through the thick humid air. It's almost Christmas again, a far different Christmas than the Christmas I spent in Alaska. It's probably near zero there or below by now. Here in South Vietnam, it's eighty-four degrees. Vietnam has two seasons, wet and dry. The cold season runs from November to April, the hot season from

May to October, here in South Vietnam, the temperature differences between the two seasons were barely noticeable.

The morning sun had crested, casting a red fog that filtered over the mountains in the remoteness. The sky was one worthy of painting, reds, and oranges with almost white streaks filling the heavens. From up here, a pale gray mist floated over the jungle canopies below. The green of the open valleys consisted of scattered trees and tall bushes. The small steams reminded me of the fresh water creeks we had back home.

We spotted three large elephants, (con voi) below us at one point as they grazed in a field; they were feeding off a large clump of trees, brush, and scrubs. A smile crossed my face, I was glad I didn't have to pick up any elephant shit.

SGT. Layton had been reading a letter from his Aunt Francis telling him that his Uncle James had died, she wanted to know if he was coming back home for the funeral. We could not hear over the noise of the chopper from where he was sitting, so he moved to a closer seat.

"I need to ask you a question." He shouted leaning in, "I don't want to go back home! What should I tell her?"

Having no idea what to say, I just said it. "I have no idea!"

"Well, you're not any fucking help!" He screamed at me, and then settled back in the seat.

Unexpectedly, round streaks of light began flashing through the thin skin of the helicopter across the right side. Seconds later the reality of what was happening sunk in. The shafts of sudden light were bullets ripping through magnesium skin of the Huey! The pilot pushed forward on the cyclic stick heading for the deck, as more rounds tore through the back of the ship. I saw blood splatter from Joseph's chest, he went down falling onto his right side, blood began to puddle under him!

Panicked, and with no rational thought left, I picked up our field radio turning it on! I had no idea who I was about to call or who would hear my transmission, but I was calling some damn body! At that point, I was hit bloods suddenly all over my face! The more I wiped the more blood I had on my hands! From all of the blood on my hands I believed I had half my face blown away! I didn't want to die! Again, I wiped my face with my right-hand trying to figure out where I was, hit. However, I could not find the wound! Still! There was more blood! I started to cry as my emotions were running away with me; Joseph was still down and bleeding!

Layton went down on his knees in front of me holding to whatever he could find to stabilize himself.

The pilot is rocking the chopper violently trying to evade any farther gunfire; we fought to get onto our feet, which proved useless.

Layton grabbed my right hand pointing to my fingers. "They hit you in the hand!" He's screaming!

It took a while of turning and twisting my hands to figure out what he was saying. Then I saw the wound, a bullet had passed through my index finger as well as the finger next to it. It happened so fast I didn't feel it. I thanked God it wasn't my face.

The pilot is fanatically pushing and tugging at the controls causing the ship to go to the left then right as we descended. The doors were, closed, and we could have been, tossed out for sure. I tried reaching Joseph to see how badly he was hurt, yet the reeling and rocking of the helicopter, was so unstable I could not get to him without falling on him. At the same moment, Layton is trying to bandage, my hand with a maintenance rag he found on the floor of the chopper!

Rounds were still hitting and cutting through the chopper, outside smoke and flames were leaping across the doors and windows. Then about two-hundred and fifty-feet above the ground, all hell broke loose. They hit us with something large, perhaps twin 50's. The ship was, hit just behind the fuel cell taking out the hydraulics. We were going down.

We managed to escape the flames for now, but the smoke was thick, black, and choking inside the cabin! We fought fiercely to hold on while fighting to catch our breath!

The pilot into the radio, "May Day! Mayday! Home Nest, this is Recon Zulu - Over."

All at once, everything electrical died including the radio, the large gun had hit its target. Panicked we struggled to hold on to anything that we could.

With the engine failing, the centrifugal clutch released its grip, letting the blades turn freely, powered only by the wind now! The pilot used the collective stick to add pitch giving him the ability of increasing or decreasing the cut of the blades slicing into the wind, slowing or advancing our, decent as he needed. The cyclic stick now free to push the squash plate in any direction needed, it was apparent the pilot was doing everything he could to get us on the ground safely.

I saw a truckload of enemy soldiers coming toward us as we were going down; suddenly trees seem to come out of nowhere! Then came the nerve racking sounds of the, *'Crash!'* Pieces of the helicopter and one outer door were broken away from the craft. Like shrapnel, pieces and bits were, thrown in every direction. Hitting the ground, the rotor blades dug their way into the soil and grass, she was coming apart. I was, tossed out of the helicopter into the air. My body was tumbling through the sky like a football! All I could see was the heavens, trees, ground, and then more sky and trees. All at once, wham! I landed on my back with my breath knocked out of me, but at least I was alive. I lay there, gasping like a fish out of water. Then came the explosion, the burning rubber fuel cell had exploded sending flames wildly into the air only to be followed by a large bloom of black smoke.

SGT. Layton was suddenly in my face, "You all right!" He screamed.

By this time, I'm breathing shallow breaths.

"Ok," being all I could muster.

Layton helped me into a sitting position; he had cuts and abrasions to his face and chest, but seemed to be moving ok. "Neither the pilot nor the crew-chief made it!" His voice hastened.

Setting there, I could see that Sims had made it out uninjured; he was at Joseph's side working on him. Though we had all been crossed trained as medics, our first objective was to the mission which came first above all else. If a, man were hit, he was left for the moment until the area had been cleared of any enemy. Once the area is secure, we will attend to the wounded. Here, the mission had been a total wipe, now the mission had become a matter of just staying alive.

Finally, I managed to get to my feet.

"You hurt?" Layton said picking up the field radio, "Other than your hand?"

"No, I just got the breath knocked out of me," I finally managed to say in a complete sentence.

We heard the approaching truck in the distance that I had seen while we were going down, yet we could not see it, but I knew the truck was nearby. "We gotta' get the hell outta here!" I warned.

Handing the radio to me, "Here, take this," Layton rushing off to help Sims with Joseph.

I headed for the tree line that lay some thirty-feet away only to stop. My training had finally kicked in.

I quickly removed my pack, took out a claymore. Placing it facing the burning helicopter, I attached a trip wire to it. Then I went about stomping a path in the grass making it appear that once out of the helicopter we ran straight for cover in the trees.

Layton and Sims were carrying Joseph; they had his arms draped over their shoulders with his feet dragging across the ground behind him. He was alive but unconscious. Once we got to the trees we spread out, we took turns checking our weapons. The truck was closing in.

In a matter of seconds, we saw two VC in the front seat with six more in the back of the truck clinging to the side rails. All of them dressed in black pajamas. This would be our first encounter with the dreaded Vietcong. My hand bled as I held to the trigger of the K-9 with blood dripping from my fingertips. The cloth had fallen off during the confusion; fortunately, the excitement of the moment had taken away the pain.

Making ready, SGT. Layton moved to my side with his M-16 at the ready. SGT. Sims turned to us, holding a compress to Joseph's ribs. "His blood pressure is dropping, who has the Hespan? We are going to lose him!"

"I got it!" Layton shot back digging the medical kit out of his rucksack, finding the Empiric Bolus; he tossed the sealed bag over to Sims.

Joseph's blood systolic pressure had dropped below fifty to forty-four. Sims started an IV of 1000cc's of Hespan in an attempt to bring him back.

The group of men had overheard us. Here they came. Everything is happening in seconds; finally, we had caught a break. They found the fake trail. Following the path straight the claymore, and the, *'Blooommm!'* The claymore exploding spewing small ball bearings and plastic pieces tearing and ripping their flesh; followed by a shower of blood. Four bodies floated backwards in the air for a split second before hitting the ground. The remaining four Vietcong scattered. Two of them began firing wildly into the trees at us as they ducked for cover. Some distance behind the smoldering Huey. The remaining two began blindly shooting at us in an attempt at hitting us hiding in the thick foliage. Spraying and praying as it were. Thankfully, they didn't know our exact location. The other two headed toward their truck with Layton following them with gunfire from his M-16. He hit one of them in the back, he went down, but his quick thinking partner took refuge behind a small hill near a single standing tree.

"Does anyone know if the ELT (Emergency Location Transmitter triggered upon impact) is working?"

Sims moving to my side, "I have no fuckin' idea, I hope its working!"

Layton is keying up the field radio, "Home Nest, this is Recon Zulu - Over!"

Followed by Static.

"Home Nest, this is Recon Zulu - Over!" Layton repeated.

"This is Home Nest Recon Zulu. What is your situation? - Over."

"We were shot down twelve miles northwest on route to Tay Ninh Province. Mission number is MA8872. We have three men down, two dead, one wounded. Five Enemies are down, three-alive - Over."

"We have a fix on your locator; help is on the way - Over!"

"ETA? - Over."

"Twenty-five minutes! I repeat, twenty-five minutes - Over!"

"Roger Home Nest - Over and out." Layton putting the hand set away. "If one of those bastards makes it back to the truck, they will radio for help," Layton warned.

In almost the same moment while Layton was on the radio, I had checked on Joseph, he was stable thanks to Sims. I prayed that Joe would regain consciousness soon.

Returning to SGT. Layton and Sims, "We need to take them out."

Layton pushing, a fresh clip into his M-16. "Let's do it!"

I got to my feet taking two grenades from my ammo belt, not understanding what he had said. "Okay!"

"You can't reach them from here! You crazy?"

"I can if you and Jimmy give me some cover fire, I'm going to the front of the chopper by way of a small hill down there," I pointed.

"Go for it," Layton said.

In front of the helicopter, was a clump of brush and a small rise in the earth with a sloping hill on the other side? I moved down the tree line to the far right while making my approach far away from the others. Once I got into position, I waited for the signal. As Layton, and Sims opened up with their M-16's, I began running for the smoking Huey. Diving I landed on my belly. I used the helicopter's position to my advantage. I pulled the pin on the first grenade, making a poolroom bank shot off the damaged rotor blade. The grenade bounced off the backside of the blade that had stuck into the ground upon impact, landing on the other side of the chopper near to where two VC were taking refuge.

Just as Layton and Sims ran out of ammo with each of them scrambling to reload, our training broke into my thoughts. We had been trained for this kind of situation, we didn't fire together but rather covered the other teammate while he was firing. The other team member would then fire while the other is reloading. The whole idea was to keep the enemy pinned down, something we had practiced repeatedly. However, this was the real thing, not training; we had allowed panic to intervene. Because of this mistake, the two VC scrambled for their truck in an attempt to gain the upper hand. My grenade exploded sending shrapnel in every direction, normally the grenade would have killed or injured both of them, but because of this error, only one of them went down. Layton fired cutting the other man down in mid-stride.

The force of his body's forward-motion, and the bullets slamming into his back sent him into the air for about five-feet before hitting the ground. Layton came rushing down the dirt bank toward the truck with Sims' on his heels. I came out from behind the helicopter with my K-9 spitting at the remaining Vietcong. They had a fixed machine-gun mounted on the bed of the truck; the lone survivor was heading straight for it!

"Grenade!" Sims shouted as the grenade left his hand.

We hit the ground covering our heads with our arms. The grenade landed at the front of the truck, three seconds later, the grenade exploded flipping the truck over onto its right side rolling onto the bad guy crushing him beneath it. After checking to see if he was dead, we began making our way back to check on Joseph. We found the wounded VC wounded by my grenade. He was groaning but alive. Lying at a tree near the downed chopper, Sims moved in taking his weapon. The little man is in pain from his injuries.

"Go check on Joseph," I directed Sims, taking the confiscated AK from him.

"You are going to kill him?" Layton, questioned.

"No, I'm gonna see if I can help him. Look how young he is."

I took out a Morphine Serette, (Morphine with a Disposable Needle) removing the protective cap and gave him the shot in his leg to ease his pain.

Frightened and hurting, he tried getting away from me as I gave him the injection. "Ban ten gi?" (What is your name?) I asked.

He is sweating, twisting, and turning on the ground like a wild animal, "Tôi se giet ban!" (I will kill you) he answered.

The Morphine began taking effect; slowly he began to settle down. He started smiling and talking nonsensically. I took the top off my canteen and poured some water into my hand and rubbed it on his face, even though he was afraid, he let me do it. "Nuoc?" (Water) I asked offering the canteen.

He nodded yes so I put the canteen to his lips but allowed him only a small swallow. His stomach wounds were serious, and I didn't want to kill him.

He was our prisoner, under the laws of the Guevara Convention; we were bound to care for him until he could be, turned over to the proper authorities for questioning. Finally, he relaxed and let me examine his stomach wounds. He allowed me to apply a compress to help slow his bleeding.

Looking at Layton, "Can you watch him while I check on Joseph?"

I walked up the slight hill to Joseph. SGT. Sims had him sitting up and talking while checking the bandages on his chest. Going down on one knee, "How's it going, buddy?" I asked.

"Fine," he groaned and then coughed a few times while holding to his side. "I missed all of the action."

"You have had plenty of action, trust me."

We heard two Huey's approaching from the south. Sims and I got Joseph to his feet, carrying him in a chair like cradle. We started for the tree and the prisoner, the pain in my hand reminded me that I needed to attend to it. We made it back to Layton where we positioned Joseph so he could sit back against the base of the tree next to our captive.

SGT. Layton and I went to the Huey, where we removed the pilot and the crew chief's body, placing them near the prisoner.

All of us were in a semi-state of shock. It was the first time either of us had seen dead people burnt and blown apart. This was completely different than seeing my Dad in a casket when he died.

I had to fight back the childhood fears of the dead coming back to life and going crazy striking out at any and everything that moved as I had seen in the movies.

As both Huey's landed, two-medics appeared from the first one carrying a stretcher with them while we went about getting Joseph ready for it. We told the medics what we had done for him so far. After they inspected the wound, they attached a fresh IV, and then rushed off back toward the helicopter.

"Where are you taking him?" I asked.

"Will be in touch with your company," one of them said over a shoulder as they scrambled away.

I thought it odd that neither of them had so much as glanced at our prisoner.

A Marine Lieutenant from the second chopper walked up to us, addressing, SGT. Layton, pointing to the wounded man. "What is this?"

"Sir, we managed to capture a prisoner," Layton speaking up proudly, walking with the Lieutenant back toward the tree, "He looks, awful young, Sir." Layton added.

Layton, Sims and I stood there waiting for the Lieutenant to say something, but without a word, the officer removed his forty-five from his holster and shot the boy twice in the head.

"Sir! We captured him!" I said. "He could have known something!"

The Lieutenant looked at me. "Next time you idiot's capture an enemy, check his body for weapons!"

I stood mute.

He returned his weapon to its holster. "Check his right hand!"

I checked his hand as ordered; he held a semi-automatic pistol cocked and ready to fire.

The Marine Lieutenant just saved our young naive asses.

They had a name for us new people, no matter how much training we had, no matter how well we handled ourselves in the field, we were Cherries with a capital C. As a warrior, like the millions of warriors over the centuries, we had our very first baptism under fire. A social intercourse with war, our Cherry had been broken. How would we handle it and what it would mean to us this day as well as beyond, was still to be determined? We no longer referred to the Vietcong as bad guys. From now on, they would, be called, Gooks, Charlie, Chuck, or Charles.

"All right men, get your gear and climb aboard, we'll drop you off at Tay Ninh Province, Zulu One. It's on our way."

"Yessir," we said one after the other Huey.

*Ian Smith in order to prevent a
majority black rule declares unilateral
independence for Rhodesia*

CHAPTER SIX

THE DUMBEST PERSON I EVER MET: Thirty-minutes later, we had gathered our gear and climbed aboard the Marine's chopper, for the remaining leg to Tay Ninh Province. A helicopter was coming from another nearby Fire Base for removal of the dead flight crew. They would also insure that nothing of interest to Charlie would be, left behind.

The first thing I noticed was the fact this pilot handled the flight pattern of this Huey much differently than his protégée had from this morning's flight. It was evident this pilot knew what he was doing. He stayed about eight-feet above the treetops keeping the chopper's forward air speed around eighty-knots. Over the rice paddies, he dropped down to eight feet again. We did pass some farmers working in the paddies from time to time. Yet they were only blurs and then they were gone. Anyone down there trying to get a fix on us would have one helluva of a time locking on. Only because by the time spotted us, we would be gone. The wind coming through the open doors was cooler since the air had dried out somewhat becoming less humid.

Layton caught me staring at the pack of beef jerky he was working on...

"You want some?" He yelled over the, Huey's noise moving into the seat next to me, I couldn't hear him, but his hand gesture made it clear what he was saying.

Taking two of the offered strips, I tore off a piece and began chewing. It was soft, fresh, and easy to eat; it tasted kind of like three-day old steak. I had a regular bottle of Coke in my pack, popping the cap off with my knife blade I took a long drink. Having no way to keep it cold, it foamed up inside my mouth so much I had to hold my nose. I offered Layton a swallow of it, but he refused. I guessed the idea of possible beef jerky backwash had turned him off. Sims opened his pack, retrieving several chocolate bars offering everybody on board one, including the pilot and crew chief. The three Marines along for the ride brought out brown rice and two packs of C-rations. Before we knew it, we had a regular feast going on. The pilot told the crew chief to bring out the case of beer from the floorboard where the copilot would sit if there had been one. A square metal toolbox served as an ice chest, it was full of ice-cold cans of Pabst Blue Ribbon. He passed them around until everybody had one.

Twenty-minutes later, we were entering Zulu One's air space. A group of Marines below had gathered to welcome us, popping green smoke (Safe Landing Zone) which began twisting and curling into the air from our prop wash. The pilot turned the chopper sideways causing us to drift in descending gently onto the landing pad carved out of the dirt below us. Once down the pilot cut the engine as we climbed out. We spotted the other four-man Recon Ranger Team, the three of us gathered on them.

We were, greeted with smiles and handshakes as we approached, "Hi, men." SGT. Blevins a tall lanky man from New Jersey said. While passing out a copy of the mission map to us. "I'm Squad Leader and being so means that I am in charge of this mission, as I'm sure you have been apprised. My team will lead the way doing the mission the way I see fit. Is that clear?" He smiled he had enough teeth for another mouth.

There are people you meet in life who you take an immediate disliking. This guy was at the top of my list. His behavior told me that the wheel was spinning, but the hamster was asleep. I suppose making snap judgments about anyone could be rude and very insensitive, but it was the way, I had perceived the guy.

Layton leaning in behind me, "I see the man has a God complex, this should be interesting."

Others rolled their eyes indicating to Layton and I that we were not that far off base.

Lt. Williams was on his way to where we had gathered from his command shack. He walked up to us stopping just short of the group.

SGT. Blevins snapped to attention. He saluted as the Lieutenant neared us. "Lt. William's Sir, Sergeant Blevins reporting as ordered, sir."

"Put your goddamn arm down Sergeant. You trying to get me killed?"

"No Sir!"

"You've made this greeting for the fifth time today; I think I know who you are by now!" Williams cracked.

"Yes Sir."

"All right people, this way," Williams turned and headed for the ridge near the end of the clearing some fifty-feet away. Once we were there, he pointed straight out in front of us. "The area you are to Recon lays five-miles' due east of here. You are to encircle the hill you see just past that far ridge, and then turn back to Camp Minh to the south. The locations are marked clearly on your mission map. SGT. Story will meet you there, once there, you are to spend the night. Tomorrow morning you are to go south two miles and report back here completing your mission. You should be back here about 1300 ZULU tomorrow afternoon."

Each of us had a copy of the map out studying the predetermined route as he had read it off. Yessir," we answered collectively.

Lt. Williams walking away, "Good luck," he said as he headed back to the command post.

"Yes Sir, thank you Sir," Blevins said. "All right people', I'm taking point, I need a slack man."

SGT. Sims stepped forward, "I got it," he said.

Blevins eyed him for a moment before agreeing. "Good, let's move out gentlemen."

Two of Blevins men, SGT. Black, and SGT. Bowers moved behind Sims taking up a watchful position, Layton and I fell to the end of the column taking the rear lookout with SGT. Bicks.

Together we stretched the column out avoiding bunching up, being careful to maintain our intervals.

SGT. Bowers' the TL Team Leader stands six-foot, blue-eyed with brown hair. Has that country boy look about him, he slowed falling in line next to me. I gathered he was looking for his proper place in line, I guess everybody had their preference; mine was bringing the rear.

No one spoke, we used arm and hand signals to communicate, while moving as quietly as possible. We were all greener than grass, but this day we thought of ourselves as professionals Our training kicked in; we searched the ground for anything unusual as we went, careful to stay in the shadows moving as though our very lives depending on where we placed our next step, as if we knew what we were doing.

SGT. Blevins is still at point, moving along as if he didn't have a care in the world. He would stop at different times looking back at us,

We were moving into thicker trees, the overhead tree canopy had begun to thicken, making it darker on the forest floor. From Sims on back we stopped the chatting and gave our attention to our surroundings. Blevins on the other hand never broke his stride. After moving another mile, he had stopped, taking a seat on a dry log in a clearing where we were to turn south.

One by one, we stopped on him as they reached the clearing. By the time I got there, Blevins and another man were smoking and having snacks.

It was plain for everyone to see that Layton was pissed. Protocol had been broken. Although this exercise may be nothing more than just going through the motions, Protocol was to be, followed.

"SGT. Blevins, you're breaking Protocol by smoking!" Layton said firmly, but in a low voice.

Blevins spoke in his natural voice not caring who overheard him. "Don't get your grenades in a bunch Sarge! The United States Marine Corps cleared this area, no one's out here, everything is cool!"

Layton walked straight over to him, stopping long enough to slap the cigarette out of his mouth, "You stupid sonofabitch! If this were a real exercise you could get us all killed!"

Blevins and one of his men scrambled to their feet to face Layton. Layton knocked Blevins, comrade out, then pinned Blevins to the tree with a knife to his throat. "I've been shot at today no fault of my own!" Layton grimaced. "We're going to do this by the fucking numbers or we are going to be short one dumb ass Squad Leader you got it?" He, threaten.

Sims and I readied our weapons to back Layton's move. Blevins team members didn't offer a comment. It was plain to see Layton was correct in his convictions.

"All right... all right!" Blevins said. "Let me go."

Layton released his grip, yet held to the knife to Blevins throat as he backed away.

Blevins rubbed his throat as he put his hat back on. "I am still in charge; this, little episode of yours changes nothing!" He complained staring at Layton.

"As long as Protocol is followed, asshole, I don't care who's in fucking charge!"

Blevins straightens his clothes, and then picked up his weapon, "This isn't over, and I am putting you on report!"

With a few more splatters of a pissing contest between the two, a reluctant truce was finally, reached, so we returned to the path and headed south.

Sims returned to the slack position, yet careful to stay some thirty-feet or more from Blevins.

If anything went down, he wanted to make sure he didn't get it along with Blevins.

Two hours passed as the ever-thickening brush and vines toward Camp Minh became more difficult to walk through. Thankfully, forty-five-minutes later we came upon a small clearing in the woods. The undergrowth had begun thinning somewhat. The humidity is rapidly rising; it's evident that an oncoming rainstorm wasn't far away. After covering other two-miles, we saw the makings of a village slowly coming into view in the distance. Two Marines were standing guard as we approached Camp Minh. One was a sergeant, possibly SGT. Story who we were to report.

"You guys' Recon Zulu?"

"Yes we are," Blevins said stopping in front of the two men. "Are you Sergeant Story?

"I am," the sergeant answered.

"This is my team, where do you want us?" Blevins smirked.

Evidently, SGT. Story was not a patient man, that or either Blevins remarkable ability to piss people off had preceded him. "They're your fucking team, put them any goddam place you want!"

Layton and I left Blevins standing there conversing with the Sergeant in his blissful state of unawareness, as the two of us moved slowly into the village with Sims tagging along.

There were five considerably large hooches' scattered twenty-feet apart. Five large empty cast iron kettles sat near a burned out campfire. Two smaller kettles hung over an open flame near the entrance of the village. A small woman sat with her ass resting on the back of her heels stirring the cooking rice with a large wooden spoon, with her eyes following our every move.

Layton and I walked to the covered porch of the middle hooch standing on stilts. The thatch roof covered houses sat four-feet off the ground; the wide porch had a long bench stretching from the corner of the building to the edge of the door. We climbed the steps taking a seat on the bench. "Do you see anything wrong with this picture, the large pots, and the large but empty buildings?" Layton asked.

"The pots," I agreed, "Not only the size of these buildings, but also the lack of people. Remember our training?"

"This is a goddamn Vietcong camp!" Layton came back.

"Congratulations, you just won the teddy bear."

Layton touching my arm, "But it can't be. The Marines came through here. Maybe they killed them all?"

"They would have burned the village, not only that. However, there are no signs of a firefight.

The large pots were for cooking rice all right, and they were capable of serving at least one-hundred to a twenty-people. The hooch's were large enough to house more than fifty-people each if not more. The camp was, well maintained requiring more care than a few kids were and three old women could provide. I for one didn't want to be here when Chuck came back home.

We both saw shadows moving in the trees in the distance across both sides of the road in front of us. "Did you see that?" Layton lashed out.

"We are leaving with or without Blevins and his men," getting up from the bench. We hurried down the steps together our weapons at the ready.

Moving to SGT. Black and Bowers who was standing together at the edge of the road, "Guy's we gotta get the hell outta here, and I mean now!" I warned.

"What's going on?" Came from Black.

"This is a VC village!" I answered. "We have visitors, let's move!"

The old woman who had been stirring the rice was suddenly gone. Searching the immediate area, I realized the two younger women had disappeared as well. I wasn't waiting to be shot at, "It's an Ambush! Take cover!" I shouted.

Blevins confused, grumbling with a cigarette handing out of his mouth. "I did not order any ambush! What are you talking, about?"

Breaking the afternoon silence, two cracks from an AK-47 sent two instantaneous thuds smashing into Blevins, chest! He went down like a sack of rocks. Everyone else scattered for cover. I couldn't tell where the shots had come from; I dove in the air landing by a small scrub bush rolling into a prone position with my K-9 all set.

Sergeant's Black and Bower had run into the woods in different directions. In the same moment I heard,

SGT. Sims scream from behind me, "Layton, on your right!" He warned.

We both turned, a small figure perched behind a rock with an AK barking! Tow! Tow! Tow! The bullets hitting all around Layton.

I spotted a small woman crouched behind a stack of wood twenty-five feet in front of me, I fired in short burst hitting the woman in the head with my K-9. Her limp body fell backwards and started shuddering as she slowly died.

"Behind you!" Layton cried out to Sims. The old rice woman was on the porch firing at Sims, he turned firing back him killing her.

Getting to my feet I ran for cover landing on my stomach again, but this time taking refuge under a porch, the ground beneath me was unusually soft, and then it gave way. I had fallen into a pit, the pit's at least eight-feet deep, and twelve-feet square. There were two large cages with two huge bears locked inside them. Outside, the firefight had become more involved. The bears were lashing out at me through the bars with their large claws. To make matters worse I had landed on my K-9, it was pushing into my chest. I was so scared; all I could do was hug the ground! The shock of everything happening around me made it hard to draw details for this situation from our training! Paralyzed with fear, all I could say came out as, "Oh God! "Oh God!" My mind was racing a thousand miles a minute, it took me more than a few moments too realize I was totally out of control!

Drill Instructor Miller came crashing into my thoughts; his loud raspy voice began barking inside my head. *'The first thing that will kill you out there is fear asshole!'* He had screamed at us several times and on many occasions. *'There is no room for fear asshole! Fear is your enemy asshole! Fear is the enemy! You will not be able to see the Vietcong! You cannot see fear asshole for fear will kill you! Fear shuts down the thought process asshole! Do not! I Repeat! Do not let fear kill you! Do you understand me?"*

Under my breath, I whispered aloud. "Yes Drill Sergeant, I understand you!"

There were screams of pain and dying from both sides. I managed to step up on some crates stacked in the corner of the burrow and climb out. Using the corner of the porch for concealment, I hid for a few seconds trying to get my bearings; I heard shots fired and another one of our squad members screaming in the distance. Sounded like he had gone down just to the right of me, finally, I managed to get to my knees. There is a log under the porch in front of me, and for one reason or another, the gunfire had unexpectedly subsided. Quietly, I pushed a fresh clip into the K-9 checking the safety. I slowly moved toward the next hooch being careful to keep my distance from any more would be pits. I stopped after a few feet. Then thirty-feet in front of me I saw a black draped figure down on one knee hiding behind a decomposing post poised to take a shot. Opening up on him with the K-9, he went down quietly. It's then I heard the silence; I had never heard it so quiet. Only thing I could hear were the slow but steady falling of raindrops hitting the leaves and roofs of the hooch's overhead and the ground around me. The rain splashed on my head and shoulders, as the water trickled down my face and neck.

After twenty minutes or so of observing, I heard a faint cry to my left.

"Logan, help me!"

I didn't recognize the voice right away, slowly but cautiously I began moving in the direction of the sob for help. It took me awhile to get there because I wasn't taking any changes. Then I saw him, it was Bower lying flat on his back with his head up straining to locate me.

Carefully I moved to his side; they had hit him in the left shoulder and stomach. Pulling his shirt to one side, it was plain to see that his stomach wound was the more serious of the two. The round had entered at the top of his naval, and exited out of his lower back tearing out a three-inch hole. Revealing that his spine was blown away. There wasn't any movement from the waist down. To make matters worse, he was rapidly bleeding out, and growing weaker with every beat of his heart. I gave him three, Morphine Serrates. I was determined to help him leave this earth pain free. I wanted to tell him goodbye, yet the words just would not come.

Grabbing my arm, "My Mother is standing in the road over there Sarge," he cried pointing with a finger. "Tell her to come over here and help me!"

I looked back but didn't see anything.

With tears streaming down his face, "You see her?"

I took his hand in mine, "I see her, she's coming buddy," I lied.

His expression consumed with fear. His eyes were darting from left to right. I am scared Sarge. I don't want to die," he muttered with blood coming out of his mouth.

Suddenly, automatic fire from two-AK's opened up. The rounds hitting the ground around us tree bark, leaves, and dirt flew into the air. Bowers took a single round in the right side of his face finishing him. I was, hit in my right leg. Whoever had taken those shots was using Bower's to draw me in for the kill.

This scenario was, practiced repeatedly in our training, yet seeing Bower laying there had caused me to neglect it. Quickly, I managed to scramble away taking cover in the thick brush behind a fence. Fear, had been replaced with calmness and anger. My leg didn't hurt anymore; adrenalin had stepped in turning off the pain. I had taken the round in my right leg at the top of my long bone where it connects to the hip. The wound was too high up on my leg to apply a tourniquet, all I could do was put pressure on it. I managed to walk on it, but with a knee-jerking limp.

Suddenly, M-16 fire rang out behind me, then to my left. Layton and Sims had come along the side of the two remaining Vietcong who had fired on Bower and me, cutting them down.

Layton yelled out after the shooting stopped, "All clear!"

I wanted to believe him, but waited for a few minutes before moving in on them. Layton was on radio calling out to Lieutenant Williams for help.

"Jimmy!" I said to Sims, "We need to search the bodies." As I began, searching one of the two they had killed. "Help me with these two!"

The gore of war without going in to details was sickening as I went about doing what I had to do. I just choked it down. As I went about the business of checking the dead bodies for any information, I remembered the Incident of the armed prisoner from earlier this morning. I worked carefully to make sure the enemy was dead. Any documents, if found may be helpful to command. With nothing of interest, I moved to the next bloody body behind the rock at the mouth of the village that I had killed. Turned out to be one of the two young women we had seen when we had arrived here. The woman didn't have any documents on her either, not that she would, but we had to check.

Moving on, I found SGT. Story by the main gate discovering that he had been, killed with a machete from behind. The young VC boy who committed the act was also deceased, and even in death; he had a locked grip on the handle of the large knife. The lad had been, shot in the back, probably by his own. The bullet had passed through striking Story in his right leg...

In searching the teenager's body, I found a detailed map of Lt. Williams 'encampment. Zulu One was marked out on the map in detail. They had circled a section of it with an 'X' drawn into the center of a larger circle. Smaller circles dotted the map surrounded by the larger circle. The command center in the drawing was clearly marked, as was each structure within the encampment.

It wasn't long before we heard a helicopter coming in from the west; it fell into a, steady hover, finally landing in a small clearing down the hill not too far from us. A few minutes later, two Marines and Lt. Williams were on us.

"What the fuck happened here, soldier?" Williams asked.

"We were ambushed Sir," Layton explained.

I left Layton to tell the lieutenant what had happened. I went looking for SGT. Black. It didn't take me long to find him, his body laid just off the road on an embankment near the mouth of the village. He lay on his back with his mouth and eyes opened. He had, been shot in the back of the head. I went down on one knee, reached out and closed his eyes and mouth.

On the way back I walked up onto the porch to the woman Sims had shot. Her body hung over its edge; it's plain to see she was dead.

Hearing the cries of children coming from within, I entered the hooch with my weapon at the ready not knowing exactly what to expect. I spotted four small children huddled in one corner with an older girl standing over them. She was brandishing a knife and ready to strike if I were to get any closer. Looking at her and the children, I said the first thing that came to mind, "Tôi xin loi này xay ra, chúng tôi đang đe lai bây gio." (I'm sorry this happened, we are leaving now.)

The feeling had begun to return to my hip, the pain was returning as well. I turned and walked toward the entrance with my back to the girls. As I started down the steps, I heard the elder girl with the knife running across the floor after me. I turned catching her right hand, while grabbing her by the waist with my left hand and tossed her high over my head letting her go. Like a limp rag, she landed on her back and rolled into a fetal position. As I walked past her, she laid crying and gasping for air.

I had lost a large amount of blood, so I began making my way toward the main group.

Once aboard the Huey, we were on the way back to Lt. William's encampment. I handed Williams the map I had taken off the boy. He studied it for a few minutes. Finally realizing what he had in his hands, he immediately reached for the radio and began relaying the newfound information to his commanding officer.

Sims was busy tending to my wound while Lt. Williams had called for our extraction once we were back at Zulu One.

I discovered something back there about myself today. I loved the rush I had experienced. However, I am afraid to tell anyone. The adrenaline gave me power over my fears in the end; maybe it was the situation of kill or be killed that did it. Whatever it was, I felt alive for the first time in my life. The danger intrigued me, and the reality of it thrilled me.

We off loaded from one helicopter onto the outbound craft, I was carried by stretcher to the waiting copter. The Morphine Sims had given me had eased the pain. Once in the extraction chopper another person started a fresh IV of Saline.

I had some cooked rice in my backpack which I had already began eating. Layton finished off another piece of beef jerky before handing me a piece. The water I had in my canteen was warm, but at least it was wet.

To Help in the Fight against Communism, Philippines President Elect Ferdinand Marcos announces he will send troops into South Vietnam

CHAPTER SEVEN

A LOVE INTREST I HAD GIVEN UP: They brought me into the emergency room on a stretcher sitting it atop a Gurney. As they did, I heard non-descriptive voices. "Got a lot of blood here," someone said guiding the Gurney.

"Dog Tags read type O," another spoke up.

White clad bodies were suddenly moving all about me. Then suddenly two on either side transferred me to an examination table.

Barely conscious at the time, yet I do remember them cutting my uniform away, and the pulling and tugging to get it off my body. I remember the harsh bright overhead lights; they hurt my eyes, so I kept them closed. I could feel people rubbing against me as they scrambled around me doing what they had to do. Unexpectedly, a sharp needle was, inserted into my ass. I tried complaining about the pain, and then blackness.

* * * *

The anesthesia had left my mouth dry, looking about me, I knew I was in a hospital ward; but the drugs had left me woozy. There were patients in four of the many beds scattered about the large room. Yet something was wrong, for I was floating above one of the beds of a wounded soldier. There were two doctors and a score of nurses scurrying back and forth around him. They were shouting, and screaming orders of what to do for him. Now it is plain to see, he is dead. His eyes are, glazed over. His expression was blank.

From above and behind me a bright light began filling the oversized room. Then I saw her, a beautiful Vietnamese girl, her skin was flawless. She floated right through me as if I was not there. She descended to the dead soldier below. The light was a brilliant white. Her black spun silk hair floating. It moved as if she was swimming under water. A white flowing gown accompanied her dazzling essences housed within the bright glowing light. Then as she reached for the soldier, he sat up in bed. A ghost of himself leaving his body behind, as he smiled and reached for her hand, then, everything went black again.

* * * *

"The Vietnamese use the term *Round Eyes* when describing American women," I overheard an American nurse explain to a GI a few beds away.

I wet my lips with my tongue and then opened my eyes. I could see only her back from where I was laying, but somehow, her voice sounded familiar. I propped myself up on my elbows looking around for something to drink.

There were only two-patients instead of the 2four I had seen in the dream myself; and the one the nurse was talking to the soldier at the far end.

I grinned to myself because the air condition was on, the sheets under me felt dry. Not sticky like the bedding we had back at our apartment. There, we had to deal with the humidity as well as the heat.

The only discomfort I was experiencing right now was my leg. The leg brace they had put on me hurt, the top of it was pressing down against the center of the bandage, which pressed down on the wound. I tried bending my knee in an attempt to relieve the pain, yet the trying only caused more pain at the top of my hip.

A Vietnamese nurse saw me looking around, and then came to my bedside. She wasn't as beautiful as the girl in my dream was, but she was very pretty.

Smiling I said, ("Tot buoi sáng, tôi xin coc nuoc, hãy." (Good morning, I would like a glass of water, please.)

Turning to me, "I speak English," she smiled. "I will return with water," her palms in a prayer like-stance under her chin as she bowed at the waist leaving my bedside.

Moments later, she returned handing me the water. Taking another look at her, I found her to be very appealing after all, her long blazing' black straight hair flowed down her back like fine silk. Her chocolate brown eyes were bright and intoxicating.

Taking a drink of water, "What's your name?"

"Maya," she said.

I held up the glass, "Thank you, Cherry Blossom."

"What you say?"

"Your name, Maya, it means Cherry Blossom.

"Ahhh yes, thank you," her smile was sweet as she looking at me as if I were mentally, challenged.

Her English is broken as she pronounced each word as if it were a word of its own, and not spoken in a sentence.

Pointing to it, "What's the leg brace for?"

The smile leaving her face told me that she was not exactly sure of what I had asked. She called out to the American nurse still seated with the GI, "Nurse, Hawks, help please?"

At the same time other nurses were bringing a patient back to the ward, he looked to be in serious condition. He had two different IV's, one in each arm, with a urine bag strapped to the low point of his bed. He had two pillows under his head, and two more at the foot of the bed with his feet propped on top of them.

"Hey man!" He said cheerfully as they rolled his bed in beside me. "About damn time, I had someone to talk too."

Nodding, "Sergeant Logan here, I thought me and the guy at the end down there were the only two here."

"SGT. Hocus here," he shot back, "Good to meet you, Sarge, yeah, it's only the three of us, man. I have been here over a month myself."

"Have to wait to shake your hand, I'm afraid I can't get up," I replied.

"No problem, man, no problem," while squirming trying to rearrange himself.

SGT. Hocus is a large black man, his demeanor jovial, that plus like Maya, he smiled a lot.

Lieutenant Nurse Hawks turned to Mai, who in turn pointed to me; smiling.

Nurse Hawks carrying a medical tray came to my bedside. "Good morning Sergeant, how are we feeling today?"

"I've been better, Ma'am."

SGT. Hocus breaking in. "It kills me how they always say. How are, *we* doing today? *L*ike they have been wounded or something too?"

Lt. Hawks pointing a finger at him, "You behave Sergeant. Or I'll take away your sponge baths."

"Oh yes Ma'am," Hocus said. "I'll be quiet as a church mouse Ma'am. Please don't be taking any sponge baths away. I promise I will be quiet: you just go ahead with your beautiful self, do what you came to do. I'm sorry I said a word, Ma'am."

Her eyes narrowing, and threatening, "Will you, please shut up?"

"Yes Ma'am, again, I'm sorry Ma'am." Laughing she turned back the sheet covering my leg, and then sat down on the metal stool next to my bed. She placed the small metal tray she had brought with her on the table next to me.

"Let's see how this looks the day after," unlocking the brace. Using care as she began removing it, I had to turn to one side so she could take it off.

Examining the wound, "This is a little inflamed." Taking a tube of antiseptic cream from the tray, "Why don't we put a little of this on it?" She said applying a generous amount to a cotton ball. Rubbing the medicine across the stitches making sure the wound was, covered. "I'm going to give you another shot of Penicillin to make sure that we get rid of any infection."

"The brace is too tight at the top, it's pressing down on the bullet hole." I said investigating her classic oval face and her olive complexion. Which seem to come with beautiful women? Her dark brunette hair molded into a bun atop her head sitting beneath a white nurse's cap. Then it suddenly dawned on me like a ton of brick. I knew this girl, her name's Reyna Thompson; I could not believe my eyes. She had been our home coming queen and the most beautiful girl in the twelfth grade. Yet here she was sitting right in front of me, fully developed and everything. She looked more like a model than she did a nurse. Her beautiful deep blue eyes and her plush lips accompanied that still astounding figure.

"I overheard you, you speak Vietnamese very well for an American," she said while opening a new bandage.

"Thank you Lieutenant," wanting to know about the leg brace, "Do you have to put that thing back on?"

"Yes," she responded. "Your hip is in serious condition. Raising your knee or sitting up in bed could rip the internal stitches or cause further damage to the wound," answering with a puzzled look that slowly began crossing her face.

Picking up my chart, "Do I know you?"

"Maybe, you ever had your panties stolen?"

She paused, her eyes studying my face, and then came, "Jack!" Her eyes widening.

"In the wounded flesh."

"Oh my God, Jack! It's really you!" Both hands going to her face and then slapping together in front of her, "My God I cannot believe this," giving me a hug and a kiss on the cheek, "How long has it been?"

"It's been four years, maybe a little longer."

Smiling, "You're making that up!"

I laughed. "Well, in any case, it's been a long time. I'll stick with four years."

Holding my hand, "My God, really? Well, what are you doing here?"

"Being shot at."

"No silly, what unit are you with?"

"Waiting to be permanently assigned," I sighed taking another swallow of water.

"I cannot believe this, you don't know how often I have thought of you," she smiled. "Now, here you are, all muscled up and looking good. How..."

"I never thought I'd ever see you again, especially in this place," smiling. "And you, you haven't changed a bit, you're still as beautiful as ever. I still have the picture you gave me. It helped me get through more than one lonely night."

"Well thank you very, much," she smiled giving a curtsey. At that point, she caught what I had said. "Ah Jack, you were always bad, I see that nothing has changed."

"My...my..." I said, "A Second Lieutenant and everything."

She moved nervously fluttering about like a bee. She had completely forgotten to put the clean bandage on the wound.

"Look, I have to help Dr. Stalks with surgery in twenty-minutes, but sometime today I'd like to get with you, you know, fill in all of the blanks."

"Sure," I said. "But meanwhile, could I get some chow, maybe extra milk?"

Rana nodded to a nurse who had overheard, "Give it five minutes, and be mindful of that leg, I'll see you in a bit," as she left.

Maya standing by, realizing Reyna neglected to redress the wound went about the chore of doing it herself. I flinched as she reapplied more of the antiseptic with a new cotton ball. She had the whitest teeth I had ever seen. The white nurse's cap flattered her complexion, made her sexier than she already was, at least to me. She smiled for the entire time she worked on me. After applying the new bandage with utter perfection, she picked up the needle full of Penicillin, and then stuck it into my ass cheek pushing the plunger down sharply, which hurt like hell. Finished, she threw the used needle and the old bandage in a nearby trash can, and then adjusted the leg brace before putting it back on.

"Thank you, Miss Maya, it feels much better."

"How you know call me, Ms Maya?"

"I know names are very important to the Vietnamese, true?"

Smiling, "Yes, true."

"You have a secret name, a given name; I will probably never know it, right?"

"Yes, also true."

"Speaking your secret name could cause you to be unprotected against evil spirits, true?"

"Also true, you know very much about me already."

"Mind if I ask if you are the only daughter?"

"I daughter number two," smiling pleasantly. "I have no brothers, only older sister, but she lives far from here."

"Thank you for tending to my wound and for checking the brace."

"Thank you, being so kind," she said turning and walked away.

"Damn Sarge," SGT. Hocus speaking up, "I have been here over a month, and all I get is, do this, do that, and a ass-load of needles, probing, and *'shutups!'* You have been here a few hours and a wake up! And you get two nurses wanting to give you some Boom, Boom! Motherfuck, life ain't fair!"

"Easy Sarge, I've known the Lieutenant since the seventh grade, and Maya is just being friendly."

"Yeah ok, friendly, as in touch me do me!" Laughing, "Where you from, Hocus?"

"Never mind where the fuck I'm from, tell me about the lieutenant's drawers you stole!"

Still laughing, "Wasn't me, my friend, my cousin Joe did the stealing. She wouldn't date him, so he went to her house and stole four pair from her clothesline. Told everybody she left them in the back of his car. We were just kids."

Hocus turned over in bed with his back to me. "That's some sick motherfucking shit right there, man."

While I was finishing with chow, Hocus fell asleep. When I was done, I left the oatmeal on the tray; it was thick as putty and tasted like shit. Finally finding a napkin for my hands, I laid back on the pillow hoping for some sleep. However, just before drifting off Maya returned to check on me.

How you do?" Smiling.

"May I have another milk?"

"Mik?"

"Sua," (Milk). "Chocolate sua neu ban có nó."(Chocolate milk if you have it.)

"Oh so sorry, milk, I be right back," and as quickly as she had left she returned with two cartons. "I still learn how to speak English," moving her forefinger side to side, "I still not good yet."

"You're doing well, it just takes practice." I replied. When she spoke, she had this habit of using both forefingers to push her long hair back over her ears.

"My family from Mekong Delta, it sets south of here."

"I have heard of it."

"Have you gone there?"

"No, I have only been in Vietnam for four months."

"Can I ask question?"

"Sure," watching her face.

"Why soldier motion for me to come to him," curling her forefinger into a come here motion. "Why soldiers do so?"

"When you say Round Eye for example, are you being rude to the women nurses?"

"Please no, it description." She defended.

"Same with the soldiers, they are not being disrespectful when pointing a finger," reaching for her hand, taking it in mine, tenderly. "Shaking hands, it's how we greet and communicate with one another back in

America. We curl our finger that way because it means to come here. It's another way to communicate when they do not speak the same language."

"Not meant as impolite?"

"No, not impolite," trying to assure.

"Americans are very strange; I will have to get use to them and their customs. I would like to go to America one day."

"Maya, I am glad to meet you," reaching for her hand. "You are very pretty."

Suddenly taking her hand away then watching me as if I had done something wrong.

"I am sorry for shaking your hand without your permission; I didn't mean to insult you."

"Not insult, you teach me, yes?" She smiled.

"I teach you, yes."

"How do you know Vietnamese?"

"We learned it before coming to Vietnam, like you, I am still learning."

"You are very wise, good you know how speak Vietnamese."

I watched her face as she spoke; she was like a child in so many ways.

"Thank you for talking to me, you good teacher," leaning over putting a hand to my face giving me a peck on the cheek. "You are very much kind," then sped away.

Odd, I thought, you are not; permitted to touch a Vietnamese person on the head, belief was that it could take away his or her spirit. I took the gesture as an act of affection, or at least I hoped that was what it was.

Somewhere in there, I nodded off only to be awaken four hours later with a different nurse taking my vitals.

"Hi," she smiled, placing a cold stethoscope to my chest, "I need you to breathe deeply, please."

After doing the same to my back, she backed away from me pointing to the nightstand. "JSOC sent over an, AAR," (After Action Report) she said. "A clerk will be by later to pick it up."

"Thank you for telling me."

An additional nurse, an older Vietnamese woman began changing out my IV but never spoke.

SGT. Hocus was awake now; so the pair started in on him after attacking me.

My curiosity aroused. "So what happened to you?"

He couldn't sit up, so he rolled over on his right side so he could face me, "Oh Man, we were out in the boonies right, firing two-hundred pound motherfuckin' plojo's at targets twenty miles away!" His playful0 personality repeated, "Twenty-motherfuckin' miles away! Anyway, next damn thing I know, we were, told to hit the dirt! We were being, mortared! Can you fuckin' believe that shit?"

Looking for any leftover milk, "How badly were you hurt?"

Shaking his head, "I thought for sure my black ass had bought the big one," with his arms in the air pointing. "I was hit in the back and went down like a rotten peach dropping from a tree. Must have blacked right out, next motherfuckin' thing I know man; they were digging a fuckin' Buick out of my ass!"

Reyna asked seemly appearing from nowhere, "You two enjoying your selves?"

"Oh yeah," I offered. "SGT. Hocus and I are going to get some bar girls in here for some Boom, Boom, (Sex usually Four to Six Dollars) and get drunk on some Bier LaRue. (Vietnamese Tiger Beer)

Hocus laughed. "Man, I could go for a motherfuckin' sip of dat."

"SGT. Hocus, I don't want to ever hear you use that word again. Do you understand me?" Reyna stormed. "A month of hearing that word is getting on my last nerve! That word is the worst word I have ever heard in my life!" She said sternly. "Now that, that's cleared up, I can get you the beer, but the bar girls are off limits."

"You hear her, Sarge? Now she's a word policeman, and I guess we're out of luck on the Boom, Boom too."

"I need something for pain, the Boom, Boom would be great, but with this leg brace it would be difficult at best."

A look of concern crossing her face, "Are you, serious, do you need something for your pain?"

"Yeah, I could take something; it's really bothering me."

Reyna retrieved a bottle of pain pills from her pocket while pouring a glass of water with her free hand.

"You do that very well," I said watching her. It was then that I noticed her nametag for the first time. It read Hawks instead of Thompson. I had heard the name Hawks when Maya had called out to her, but it hadn't registered with me until just now.

"I bet you two have a little chick in every port?" Handing me the water then opened the bottle, removing three of the pills placing two of them into my open palm.

"Don't know about the Sarge there," Hocus said. "I have a girl back home; I don't need a girl at any mother..." Catching himself, "Motingator port."

Looking at Hocus, she went on. "Looks like Maya has taken a liking to our SGT. Logan here, he may not need another girl either," she said glaring.

Taking the pills, I washed them down with the water. "Yeah, she's sweet," I said realizing whom Reyna had married.

"You're a good man Hocus, don't hang around with this one, he'll get you in trouble."

Smiling, she took off her hat and bent over at the waist. Undoing the bun atop her head, she let her hair fall free down over her face in front of her. Then she snapped her head backwards, causing her hair to cascaded back over her shoulders in a whipping motion, throwing the bulk of it over and down her back. Strands of wild hair clung to the sides of her face and cheeks. Using her long fingers as a comb, she pushed the stray hairs back over her ears.

"I'm off duty for a couple of hours, I'll see you two later," she smiled.

Watching her had turned me on; SGT. Hocus looked at me shaking his head. I cracked a smile; I could tell he was thinking the same naughty thing I was.

Looking at the clock noting the time, I spoke up, "Lieutenant!" I called out to her. "It's after five, what time is dinner? I'm hungry again."

Turning back, she looked at her watch. "They should be bringing it around anytime."

"Good."

"Before I go," she said coming back toward me. "How is Sara?" She asked sitting next to me on the bed.

"No idea."

"I thought you two were destined to get married, what happened?"

"No, not me. She married an insurance salesman, some guy named Eddie."

"So how did you end up here? Last, I heard you were in Oklahoma somewhere."

"I was there and other places, how about you, a Nurse?"

"Is that so strange?"

"You never struck me as the nurturing type; you were so into fashion shows, school plays, and being home coming queen. Seemed to me nothing else mattered."

"After graduation, I enrolled into nursing school, while there the military came in and offered the upper graduates incentives to join the Army, so here I am."

"By the ring and the last name, I take it you followed through marring, Charles, our famous captain of the football team?"

She hung her head. "Yes."

"Are you happy?"

Her mood changed immediately. "Yes, I suppose I am."

"You either are, or you're not."

She bolted to her feet. "Look, I have to get out of here, maybe we'll talk later," she said leaving and not looking back.

"Sarge, you're fucking this up man," Hocus staring at me. "Did you see her face when she was talking about Maya? She is jealous, man. Then talking about her husband seems to really piss her off."

"What are they giving you for drugs?" I sighed. "You do know you can go to Leavenworth for dating an officer?"

"Only if you are caught man, don't pass this shit off like it's nothing." Hocus wrinkling his brow. "She's into you and the way you look at her, you're into her too."

"Reyna married her high school sweetheart, Charles. What about him?"

"Fuck him, man, he's there, and you are here. Be Jodie, take the girl!"

I laughed, "Get over it; she's married, and an officer. No way am I getting involved in that."

"That shit wouldn't stop a black man! I'd pound her fur mound in a heartbeat."

"It's not like that. Reyna and I have a history, but she made her choice. I know her husband Charles, not well, but I do know him from school."

Shaking his head, "That still wouldn't stop a black man."

"She's a friggin' lieutenant for Christ's sake! I could end up in jail."

"Doesn't matter, wouldn't stop a black man."

"Then what would stop a black man?"

"Some big ass motherfucker, excuse me, some big ass Motingator with a straight razor."

"Dinky dau," I muttered.

Grumbling aloud, "What does that mean?"

Maya came from behind a curtain. "It means you are crazy," she smiled. "The Sergeant thinks you are crazy, but a good crazy, he, like you."

"Yeah, yeah," Hocus searching her face, "When am I going to get my sponge bath?"

"As soon, you calm down."

"Calm down? If I were any Motingator calmer, I'd be in a fucking coma!"

＊ ＊ ＊ ＊

After Hocus had been, rolled away for his sponge bath, I asked one of the nurses for a notebook. Mine were at the apartment. Having a lot to say, I started this one as I had the others. I put my name on the inside front and back covers with my home address, adding instructions as to what to do with it and the others if found in case of my death.

Of all the things I had written into the journals thus far, meeting Maya had been the brightest moment. I felt an attraction toward her; I had no idea why other than, she was beautiful and sexy and I was horney. I suppose I was trying to get back at Reyna for marring Charles, I just didn't know. Seeing Reyna again had brought back those old memories and feelings I had for her sure enough. However, I had to stop thinking about her, and I was secretly hoping Maya could help me with that.

Later, I filled out the AAR as requested, listing the events as accurately as I could by detailing exactly what had happened in the field yesterday. I'm reasonably sure my condescending remarks will get me questioned. I was wondering if all Ranger Units operated this way, wondering if I had made a mistake.

In the background, Hanoi Hannah was spouting her usual dribble on the radio. I hated the bitch and I didn't even know her, but the music she played was great.

_____ *'Good evening everybody, this your, number one Enemy, and your favorite Playmate, Hanoi Hannah, your ra-*

*dio, associate. The little Sunbeam, whose scopes you would like to touch? We are ready again for another assault on your morale, seventy-five minutes of news and music. Broadcasting to our friends and our enemies (US SHIPS) in the South Pacific.' Now here's a tune from America's singing sensation, Tab Hunter, and here is his song, Young Love.*_____

Listening to the lyrics, I wasn't thinking about Maya, instead, I thought of Reyna. Reyna had passed my bed on many occasions, only to tease me. Still, the following day I had requested Maya as my full time nurse, and to my delight, she agreed.

We often talked and laughed while sharing family backgrounds and events with each other's families, like birthdays and holidays. My favorite part of the day was sponge bath time; Maya made them more and more intimate as the days passed. She liked me; I could see and feel it in her actions and emotions. I liked her as well, maybe I'm wrong in doing what I'm doing, but I'm not going to-do anything to discourage what's going on, only because I don't want to.

I have been here for eleven days. Failing to keep regular notes on purpose, because each day seemed to echo the day before, so I didn't bother listing the events.

On a positive note, SGT. Hocus and I had figured out a way to play chess today, we had the nurses move our beds closer together, placing them head to foot. In this way, we would be facing each other, allowing me to lie on my left side without causing pain to my leg. With him on his right side, and after about four games or so, we gave it up; the mental strain of it all became too much for us.

"So where did you say you were from?"

The nurses were busy repositioning our beds.

"I'm from Georgia," Hocus said. "My dad and I worked our peach orchards together, we have three of them."

"Large ones?"

"Three-hundred-aces each."

"That's a lot of peaches'."

"A lot, man!"

A Major in dress greens entered the ward at the main entrance. I didn't' see him until I heard, "Attention!" From the nursing staff, "As you were," the Major responded.

He walked as if he were marching on a parade field; he was carrying a briefcase in his right hand. His face wore an official business expression, accompanied by an aura of self-confidence. I began to get a bit unsettled, for he was coming straight at me, reaching the foot of the bed he stopped. Grabbing the medical chart from the hook on the top rail of my bed, he studied it for a moment before putting it back. I saw his nametag, Baginski.

Reyna came out of nowhere as usual.

Acknowledging her, "Lt. Hawks," as she approached.

"Major," she replied.

He turned to me. "How are they treating you, Sergeant?"

"Fine, Sir."

"How's the wound?"

"It's mending, Sir, I should be outta here soon."

"Nurse!" Back to Reyna, "Is it possible for the Sergeant here to be placed into a wheel chair? We need some privacy."

"No Sir, not possible. However, we do have couple of empty operating rooms; we can roll his bed into one of those, Sir. Just take a minute. That would assure complete privacy."

"Fine idea, Lieutenant. A-sap if you please?"

"Yes Sir."

Ran with two other nurses grabbed my bed turning it out into the aisle, and then we were off. My saline solution sloshing in its bag overhead, as the bed rolled over the uneven boards in the floor. Once in the anti-septic room, they brought in a chair for the Major where he sat with the briefcase on his lap. With the doors closed, he unfolded a pair of reading glasses and put them on. Then he began sifting through a stack of papers he had filed in folders. Finally, he removed a single set of pages from one folder, and then placed the briefcase on the floor beside him.

"Here it says you have experience as a helicopter mechanic, Sergeant?"

"Yessir, I do. Almost three years."

"You quit that to become a Ranger?"

"Yessir I did."

"Are you planning to become a hit man, maybe work for the Mob when you get out of the service?"

"I don't understand the question, Sir."

"Think about it, being an aircraft mechanic could land you a well-paying job out in the real world. The Ranger's teach you how to kill, so why the Rangers?"

"A Ranger is what I wanted to be, Sir."

Glaring, "Why is the question?"

"Why Sir? You're a Ranger; I believe you already know the answer to the question, Sir."

He just looked at me for a minute, unabated. "Tell me why Sergeant."

"Alright Sir, I wanted to be a Ranger because the Rangers have what I've been looking for."

"And that is?"

"A home sir, I can't explain it, but I feel as though I am at home for the first time in my life. I knew it when my team picked up that pole the first day of basic training. The DI's screaming at us! Then just hours into the first day, we lost twenty-one classmates because they couldn't take it. I wanted to a part of the *Best of the Best* as named by other military units. And here I am." Taking a breath, "I want to be a part of the Ranger honor bestowed to oneself as being a Ranger and all that goes with it. I want to fight for my country! I do not want to serve as cannon fodder, sir. The Ranger Creed is my life, I can recite it frontwards, backwards, sideways and upside down. I live my life by it."

"Any buts?"

"Permission to speak freely sir?"

"I'm waiting," he said.

"You read the AAR Sir? Or I'm guessing that you wouldn't be here. Three Rangers dead, protocol broken. Four of us cherries! It's bullshit, Sir! I wanted us to succeed without any member on our team getting hurt or dead. An experienced man should have been with our team, yet there were only us cherry's. I've seen combat twice, and twice I learned lessons, which will remain with me for the rest of my life. I have filed what happened out there into the CYA (Cover Your Ass) file, sir.

"I am here because of your overall scores. The AAR Report was secondary. That said. According to your report, SGT. Blevins broke Protocol from the beginning, dismissing Layton's concerns out of hand."

"Yessir."

"You and SGT. Layton followed orders as instructed by Lt. Ramsey did you not?"

"Yessir, we did."

"Then let's move on," he said, closing the subject. "I am putting together a special unit. I wanted to speak with you, SGT. Layton, Sacks, and Sims before I had to leave for Washington. Unfortunately, that wasn't possible. The unit I am assembling will be made, up of men and women of my choosing. Our missions will still come from JSOC; the only differences will be the unit will be made up of people who are willing to put the importance of the mission's first, soldiers that will do what we were trained to-do."

He had my attention.

"The unit will be the Army's version of the Marines '*CAP MOT*'. The Combined Action Platoon, the Marines has this plan on the drawing board. However, because of the goddamn bureaucrats in Washington, putting it into action could take years. The unit I am putting together will be located inside a Vietnamese village we call Heavens Alter. We can have our fingers on the pulse of the enemy. We will remain in the village and work from there until such time our individual tours end or WIA (Wounded in Action) and/or KIA."(Killed in Action). "I am offering you a place in this unit, a unit that is not based on rank, but on skill. As I have said, your overall scores were excellent; you were fifth in your class."

"Yessir, thank you sir."

Looking at me, "In the past few weeks you've taken a life or two. How do you feel about that?"

"I can't say that I had any feelings of remorse for the lives taken. When we were, shot down on the way to Tay Ninh Province. However, on the repeat mission, what happened at Camp Minh affected me much differently. I know it was a kill or be killed situation, but what bothered me was the fact that two of the women were just young girls. I left there feeling unclean."

"Unfortunately it's a part of this war, none of us like it. Understand this, the Vietcong are dedicated to being merciless even to their, own kind. They kill the old, while taking the young, boys, and girls out of the villages. Brain washing them, and training them to kill. Any of them that do not follow Ho Chí Minh's agenda are simply eliminated."

I knew he was right, I just didn't know how-to respond to it.

"I would like you to consider my unit, Sergeant. Of course, we will have new people rotate into the team at different intervals. The difference is they will train for combat before ever sitting a foot in the field. We are starting a Cherry School in two-months helping the new arrivals to be better acclimated to what transpires in field."

"Sounds good sir."

"Remember your training, Sergeant?"

"Yessir I do."

"The Cherry School will be in Saigon. The newbie will learn from the people who have been in combat; maybe just maybe we can save a few lives."

"Yessir."

"So what do you think, son? Want to be in my unit?"

"Yessir, I accept your offer."

"Then welcome aboard, Sergeant," shaking my hand. "Together we are going to kick ass, and take names out there," he smiled.

"Thank you Sir for picking me. May I ask you a question?"

"Anything."

"They had two captured bears in the village at Camp Minh; do they eat them or what?"

"Food is a possible answer; most likely they were harvesting the bear's bile, to sell it on the open market, so that they can purchase more weapons. Asians have used bile since time began as far as I know. They claim it helps to regain the eyesight, cure liver ailments, spasms, expel toxins, you name it."

"What's bile?"

"Ursodeoxycholic acid, the bear's digestive fluid, it's said to be a great energy boost as well. It's too bad you didn't kill them, they are in for a lifetime of suffering."

I nodded. "If I had known, I would have."

"Getting back to the subject, on or about the twelfth of this coming month you will be alerted. We are still going over several possible names for this Special Unit. We should have it nailed down by the time I see you again. Since it hasn't been officially approved, I trust you will keep this conservation classified?"

"What about SGT. Sacks, Sir?"

"I understand SGT. Sacks was wounded, but recovering."

"Glad to hear it, Sir, I haven't heard anything."

Once the Major had left, they returned my bed to the ward. The feeling of jubilation had over taken me; I couldn't help thinking about what the future may hold. I tried napping but I was, geared up over what the Major and I had discussed.

SGT. Hocus had, been taken back to the operating room while I had been in with the Major. The ward is empty now except for Hocus and me, who I hoped would return soon...

Almost an hour later, here came Reyna down the aisle with a lunch tray. Right behind her, they were returning Hocus to the ward. Reyna waited until they rolled his bed into place, and then went about securing the wheels before giving me the food tray. Hocus was sound asleep.

"I took the liberty of bringing you a third, chocolate milk," she said placing the tray on my lap. "It will save you from asking for it later."

Picking up the fork, "Thank you. Where's Maya?"

"She's at supply," peeking at the wound. "It looks a lot better, how does it feel?"

"Good," I stared at her nodding in Hocus' direction. "Is he gonna' make it?"

She went over to him checking his forehead with her palm; "He still has a slight fever." Then she checked his IV to make sure it was working properly, turning her attention back to me, "His wounds are serious Jack, if we can't get rid of that infection, he's not going to make it. He simply can't afford to lose any more of his remaining kidney."

"I see."

"So, tell me, how are you and Maya getting along?"

"Great, she's a great little gal."

"I guess I am a little, jealous," as she sat beside me.

"Of what?"

"Of you."

"Me, why?"

"I guess by the way she's drawn to you," shifting her weight. "We could hardly get her to say a word to the troops before you appeared, and now you can't shut her, up."

"That's good, isn't it?"

Shrugging, "I suppose."

"Joseph's here too," I added.

"Joseph! My God does the Army know about him and girls?"

"No, are you kidding?"

"Where is he?" She laughed.

"I was hoping you could help me find him. We were in a firefight up around Tay Ninh Province. He was, shot the same day that they brought me here. I haven't heard from him since then. I don't know where they took him. The Major told me that Joe was recovering, but didn't say where he was"

"Do you know his service number?"

I tore a piece of paper out of the notebook. "It's RA1479... Here you go," finishing with the number, I handed it to her.

"It's Joseph Sacks, right?"

"Yeah."

"Give me a couple of days; I'll see what I can find out."

Hocus was finally awake. "What Motingator got shot?" He grumbled in a low voice.

"My teammate."

"Aww man, I'm sorry to hear that."

Reyna got to her feet looking at her watch, then bent over giving me a kiss. "Before I go," she said to Hocus. "What's this word, Motingator that you have been saying for a while? What does it mean?"

"You really don't want to know." Hocus replied.

"Yes! I do want to know, now please, answer me."

"Well Ma'am, Motingator is a shit-load of motherfuckers."

With a frown, "I'll see you two later," she said turning back with a wave of the hand.

* * * *

The thoughts of a new duty assignment excited both, SGT. Layton and I. Layton was my only visitor since I've been here, mainly because I didn't know anyone else. There was, SGT. Sims, but he never bothered. I can't say that I blame him; hospitals are a turn-off for me as well. Layton stopped in three to four times a week, we talked, and the three of us played cards and shot the shit to pass the time.

Once I was able to get up and around, I completed the physical therapy by going for walks. I made light jogging trips around the compound trying to regain the use of my leg. It felt good to get out of this damn bed for a change; I knew I had to be careful though. I didn't want to injure myself and prolong my stay. Maya went with me on the jogs most of the time. She told the staff she wanted to make sure I didn't fall or need help along the way. I knew Reyna knew the real reason, but she didn't interfere. Oh, it was innocent enough, we only talked about things overall, mostly I tried helping her with her English. Though her accent is somewhat thick, she is doing well. On a sadder note, it made me feel bad, but I had to be honest with her. Finding a quiet place off the beaten path, I explained what Major Baginski wanted on the day of his visit. Explaining I had no idea where they were shipping us, telling her that I would probably never see her again. She fell into my arms crying, telling me, "Tôi yêu ban." (I Love You!) I kissed her, she kissed me back, and then I asked her to say it in English. Took her three tries but she finally got it out. I laughed at the way she pronounced the words. She playfully hit me because of it.

Tomorrow had finally come, they were releasing me, and all I was waiting for was the paperwork. They had brought breakfast around at 0700, but I passed on it. SGT. Layton and I were going to the mess hall for breakfast as soon as I could get out of here.

Although he wasn't here, I gave the breakfast to SGT. Hocus, because his appetite was as large as he was. I placed my tray right next to his so it would be there when he got back.

They had taken him back to the operating room earlier this morning. I said a prayer for him. While he was gone, mail from his family arrived so I stacked it on the table by his bed. I would stop bye later and visit with him.

I had already dressed myself in a fresh uniform complete with all of the accessories of whom, SGT. Layton brought over with him.

I had wanted to tell Maya goodbye, but she was with her mother at Long Binh and would not be back until later tonight.

Another thirty minutes passed before Reyna finally brought the release form, "Thank you for bringing this."

"No problem," she said, taking back the clipboard. "I'll walk you out." Passing the first set of doors, we stopped, "SGT. Layton," Reyna said. "Can we have a minute?"

Layton feeling like a third wheel, "I will meet you at the mess hall," turning to leave.

"Roger," my attention went directly back to Reyna. "This may…"

"Good news concerning Joseph," she broke in. "He's in Da Dang; he has recovered nicely and will be back here sometime this afternoon or tomorrow."

"That's great Reyna, thank you."

"I hate telling you this, but Hocus didn't make it, Jack," she said grimly.

Suddenly, I was, paralyzed. I didn't want to believe it.

"We could not stop the infection, I am sorry."

"Jesus Christ, he was a good man."

She put a hand on my face. "I know," then she kissed me on the lips.

I didn't kiss her back. I wanted to grab her and hold on to her with all of my might, but I didn't. Instead, I backed away, "I wish things were different," I said looking into her eyes, "but they aren't."

"But things are different; I just don't know how to do this. Maybe one day soon we could talk about it."

I took her left hand kissing the back of it, and then let go. I just turned and walked away. She stood in the open doorway watching me as I left, I could feel her eyes on the back of my head, but was determined not to do anything about it. Besides, the feelings I had for Maya were slowly chipping their way into my heart.

After a late breakfast, Layton and I returned to the apartment, he went to supply, while I started squaring away my equipment and made my bed.

Duty done, I just laid around for a bit before deciding to do some pushups, pull-up's, that and lifting a few free weights we had bought when we first moved in. That was short lived, the three weeks in the hospital had left me weaker than I had expected. I realized I would have to take my time. My leg hadn't bothered me at all for the past few days. Except for having a little tenderness in the center of the wound itself, it was okay.

Later in the day, we got a call asking us to report the military police's orderly room, once there they returned me to active duty.

They gave orders for Layton and I to report to the mess hall at 2300 for a mission briefing. I asked what kind of mission thinking Major Baginski had blown sunshine up our skirts, only because the twelfth had already come and gone.

They just said be there at 2300, which meant they didn't know shit from apple butter about what was going on.

It was late, something after 1500 by the time I got out of the shower got dressed, and left for the mess hall. Layton and Sims were already there when I arrived. I sat my food tray down and slid in between them.

Sims was unusually quiet. "Have you heard?"

Opening my second carton of chocolate milk, "Heard what?"

"I am being transferred, I quit," he simpered.

Leaning in, "Are they discharging you?"

"No, I am being shipped to somewhere in the rear. I will be working in supplies passing out sheets and stuff. What do you think about that?"

I didn't know what to say, so I just said it. "Sorry, but I don't know what to say."

"I just can't shoot at any more kids, I can't," he mumbled. "I hope you and Andy understand."

Layton looking at him, "We understand; if you need anything, let us know."

Chapter Eight

BIRTH OF SIRRENDER OR BLEED: The time had finally come, it was 2230 and Layton and I headed for the mess hall as ordered. I had never seen so many new faces. The place was buzzing with excitement as we took seats near the front. As people entered the tent, I saw Reyna walking with a group of nurses, Maya waved, and I waved in return. They moved to the rear taking a seat with the other medical staff that had already arrived.

Twenty-more minutes passed then even more people came strolling in. Suddenly, Major Baginski followed by a lieutenant with a sergeant at his heels walked in with paperwork in hand. He had not lied; here he was in living color.

"Attention!" Someone yelled as we snapped too. Excitement is in the air. It reminded me of an old time tent meeting. The one where those preachers with the weird hair preached fire and brimstone sermons when I was a boy back on the farm.

Major Baginski took the podium on the small makeshift platform at the front of the mess hall. "Ladies, Gentlemen, please be seated!" He began. "Every man and woman in this room knows me. I have met everyone here personally at least once. Some of you twice, each of you know why we are here," he said. "Some of you will not make it, mainly because all of my opinions regarding you joining this unit were based solely on reading your profiles, and meeting you in person. In some cases, I made decisions based on what others have told me about you. As we get to know each other on a more personal basis, our true personalities will eventually emerge. As they do, anything short of excellence, and mission accomplished from this day forward ever surfaces from any of you, then that person will be dismissed."

Baginski pointing to the Lieutenant, "Our next speaker is Lt. Higgins; listen carefully to what he has to say."

A Corporal began walking down the aisle between the tables passing out SOB insignia's. There were two in each package, one brass for our dress uniform, and one black for our fatigues.

Lt. Higgins, a tall thin man moved to the podium. "Troops," he said. "Listen up! I welcome you to the Ranger Covert SOB Special Operations Tactical Unit. We will call ourselves SOB's from this day forward."

We exploded with cheers and, "A men's!" Having no idea what he was talking about, but it sounded good.

"What does SOB, stand for?" He asked. "Where did it come from you say? It comes from the Letter E from the third line of the Ranger Creed. It begins, and I quote: *'Surrender is not a Ranger word.'* So taking that as an inspiration, we came up with this Motto when facing our enemy. SOB stands not for Sonofabitch as some of have said on more than one occasion…"

We burst into more cheers accompanied by some wolf calls!

Higgins waited until we had quieted down. "It Stands for: *'Surrender or Bleeeeed!'*" He screamed! "You can add motherfucker in there if you want to! Welcome to SOB, Soldiers!"

The screams and shouts of enthusiasm were so loud you couldn't hear yourself think! God we were we pumped!

"Some of us are still assigned to Field Force Vietnam, a provisional corps command created temporary for control of activities of U.S. Army ground combat units. Then there are those of you that are currently on TDY status. All of you are now, geminately assigned to SOB. As you already know," Higgins continued, "We Rangers are organized as independent companies: C, D, E, F, G, H, I, K, L, M, N, O and P. With one exception, J Company or Juliet, Juliet has been retired up until now because of actions in World War II that we will not get into at this time. We are rebirthing J Company for the duration. Juliet will be SOB's Company until further notice."

Finished, Higgins stepped aside, bringing SGT. John Savage to the podium, an Australian MERC (Mercenary).

"A bright hello to all, of the Sheila's and you Mates alike. My name is SGT. John Savage; I am a praetorian from down under. Australia for you Mates who don't know where down under is," pausing amid more cheers. "I am, akin to your American bounty hunter of the old west, the only difference being, I get paid more!"

We cheered and laughed wildly.

"I have been in this country since 1959. I will be here when you Mates are, back home pumping gas. Humping your wives, and raising your own little team of Rangers!"

The Cheers turned into screams of... "Hell Yeahs!"

He held up his hands signaling the all quiet. It took a few minutes for everyone to settle down.

"From this day forward, we are operating as a Covert Black Ops Team, we answer only to our Company Commander, Major Baginski!"

A-mid more screams of joy.

"That said our orders are as follows. At precisely 0500 tomorrow morning there will be fourteen Egg Beaters (Slang for Huey Helicopters) roll in here. Your gear and you will be on those beaters as quickly as possible. They will depart in groups of four at a time for our new camp located two hours north of here by truck. All medical staff and equipment will wait for two-Shithook's (Chinook Helicopters) and then follow. They will join us there when the advance team meaning *'we'* of course; pitch in and help with the unloading and placement of such staff and equipment. You got that?"

"Yes Sergeant!" We answered in unison.

"I cannot hear you, Mates!"

"Yes Sergeant!" We screamed at the top of our voices.

Savage motioned to a Staff Sergeant posted by the main entrance. "Mate, bring it in!"

The Staff Sergeant opened the double doors; and a line of soldier's began filing in. Carrying metal tubs of ice and beer and platters of mixed foods, "Welcome to SOB, Mates!" He yelled. "Dismissed! Enjoy yourselves!"

* * * *

0500 the following morning, we were standing by with gear in hand as ordered, some of us nursing our headaches from the night before. Four Huey's in a row came in at a time, the Whop! Whop! Whop! Of the blades pounding! My head was throbbing with each loud Whop!

The birds were incredibly loud and close together. Each of them floating just inches above the ground like giant dragonflies, fifteen of us at a time climbed in, no sooner said than done, we were airborne. This process continued until the last Ranger had been loaded and deployed.

Once arriving at our new home, they assigned us to twenty-man sized quarters at the rear section of the compound which over looked a waterfall to the north. The supply depot, and the mess hall was in the center of the camp; we helped to stock the Supply Quarters first, sheets, blankets, fatigues, boots, shoes, hats, helmets, T-shirts and so forth. For the newly constructed mess hall, there were new tables, chairs, benches right down to the last pot, plate, fork, spoon, and knife.

The Chinooks finally arrived in late evening with their own crew; they went about the task of erecting and furnishing the M*A*S*H Unit. Of course, we helped in positioning all of the medical equipment; this was by far the toughest tasks since they were the heaviest to move. Everything had a place, and our responsibility was to make sure that everything was in that place. They held off bringing in the medical staff until everything had been completed, although, Dr. Major Harris did come in to supervise the placement of the medical components.

Our new Unit was, positioned close to the mountain region a few miles south of the A Shau Valley Region in I Corps. In 1960, SGT. Savage with his crew had taken over an abandon church and out buildings that the French had constructed and abandoned after years of living here.

Savage had a loyal band of Vietnamese followers who named the village, 'Heaven's Alter'. Complete with a Buddha Shrine. The village members grew from a few to a hundred-and twenty-five strong over time. His people were in charge of running everything that supported this latest project for Major Baginski, and of course paid for by the US Government. The women were responsible for the cooking, cleaning and laundry if old enough the children did what they could to help. The men were responsible for building, repairing, and upkeep, while providing security for the compound.

The average age here was thirty-five. The women out numbered the men because the Vietcong had taken the men from their villages at a young age. Some of the girls managed to escape. Others were, raped or just killed outright, while even more were, left for dead. The few who were fortunate enough to make it out found their way here. I was sure each of them had a different story to tell; I wished I had the time to hear and write them all down.

Savage loved the Vietnamese people; his only motive was being able to provide a safe haven to those who wanted it.

They loved him like a father, they treated him, and us like royalty. In a matter of a couple years,' SGT. Savage and his people had made vast improvements to the encampment.

The base itself sat at the highest point in the region. The trees and the jungle canopies made it impossible to spot from the air. Water sits on three sides with the opened end of the encampment being a valley so deep, no one could climb or breach it.

The only way in or out was by air, they conducted all entries and departures under the concealment of fog, rain or darkness when possible. On clear day's entries or departures were made either at the break of dawn or at sunset. Every step had, been taken to insure the camp's safety.

Almost twenty-three hours later and done, Layton, and I returned to our quarters hoping for some sleep. We were exhausted, neither of us had gotten any sleep from the time they had discharged me from the hospital yesterday morning. Not to mention the fact that we were, up all night celebrating our new home to be.

Returning to our barracks, we had two surprises. Joseph had come in without either of us seeing him; there were more than enough smiles, handshakes and hugs to go around. The second surprise was the fact we had been, issued new camouflaged uniforms and new floppy hats. We also had the latest jungle boots, two pairs each. We were delighted. They had reissued a new genuine K-Bar. It was the standard issue Tanto knife for the US Rangers, the perfect killing weapon. It's equipped with an epoxy powdered coated high carbon steel eight-inch blade. It come stock, sharpened to a twenty-degree angle on the cutting portion of the blade, with a two-inch serrated edge at the top of the blade. Topped off with an oval shaped Kraton D thermo plastic elastomeric handle, powdered metal butt caps, with a carbon steel guard standard. Carried in a Kydex sheath, an overall length of 12 7/8 inches from its butt to the tip of its blade, it gave me an erection just to hold it.

* * * *

0700 Command Planning and Briefing Center
MISSION: MA8934 BLOODY MOON

All of us gathered for the first time at our new headquarters. SGT. Savage although Australian wore the same uniform as we did, he could have worn civilian clothes if he wanted. He had long since left the Australian Army, but kept his Sergeant title. He stood at the planner board in silence as we filed in seating ourselves. Once we were, settled, he began.

"Mates," Savage said looking at each of us in turn, as he spoke. "I have named this mission Bloody Moon, simply because the bloody moon will be bloody full while on this bloody ass mission tomorrow night."

We sat listening intensely to his every word, accordingly. The A Shaw Valley region was the setting for much fighting. Overtime, the valley received a fearsome reputation for soldiers on both sides. Our Intel revealed that a Navy pilot had been, shot down during the bombings over North Vietnam; the bombings had started back on 7 March 1965. The Navy continuing with their missions from then until present day. Commander Shore on 16 August 1966 after a month of no contact from the Commander was, listed as MIA. (Missing in Action) He had been flying an armed 4C Sky Hawk, a very dependable plane; it was his eighth routine reconnaissance mission just over the northern portion of the DMZ. His plane was equipped with the Navy's survival kit, including a transponder giving his location and a field radio for communicating with his ship. Yet, no one had reported so much as a whisper from the Commander.

Intel reports from, ARVN (Army of the Republic of Vietnam) units in the area had reported seeing an American prisoner matching Commander Shore's physical description. According to their reports, he was being, held at a Vietcong strong-hole in I Corps Domain. The village lay just west of A Shau in a mountain area, near hill 937. Even if he was not a missing pilot, he was still an American. We were going in after him.

It was after six by the time the briefing was, over. The three of us, Layton, Joseph, and I went to the mess hall for chow, it was there that I felt a tug on my arm while standing in line. I turned, and it was Maya smiling as always.

Giving me a hello kiss, "We arrived this morning, we like our quarters."

"Want to join us?"

"I can't, see you later; bring you medical kit for mission?"

"Okay," I said as she gave me another kiss, and then watched as she sped away.

"Where in the hell did you meet her?" Joseph asked smirking.

"She's a nurse," Layton added.

"A head nurse, I hope," Joseph cracking a perverted smile.

"Down boy," I shot.

Layton sliding into his seat, "So what are you going to do with her?"

"Do?"

He laughed, "Besides that?"

"Let it go where it goes, what can I say, I like her a lot."

"You think that's a good idea?"

He had me there. "I don't know."

"I know," Joseph spoke up. "Let me at her."

"Why don't you pick on Reyna, she's here too?"

"Reyna Thompson is here?"

"Yeah, she's married to Charles Hawks, you remember him don't you? And on top of it, she's now a lieutenant."

She doesn't know what she wants," Joseph went on.

I just stared at him. Once we finished with dinner, we had all night and all of tomorrow to get our gear in order. The small barracks we were assigned to was more than adequate for our needs, it's comfortably housed with ten bunk beds with a window between each set of beds, larger windows on each end, and it's complete with running water and indoor plumbing, all the comforts of home.

It was past eight when Layton and Joseph went to the bar for the noncommissioned officers and the civilians on post. They were going to give me a few hours of privacy with Maya in hopes of getting lucky in their own right, while doing me a favor.

While waiting for Maya, I wrote today's events in my notebook talking about all of the work we had done here over the past few days.

By eight-thirty, I heard a timid knock at the rear door; Maya stood smiling on the other side, as I reached for her hand, and helped her step up into the room. Then closed the door behind her, she had the medical bag in one hand and two small mirrors in the other. She was dressed in an Ao-Dai, the traditional Vietnamese dress slit up the sides, worn with a pair of slacks. Her raven hair hung well below her waist, she was beautiful, and I told her so.

Holding the medical bag in her right hand, "Everything you will need is in here, a six-man Ser...Serette pack," she stuttered, "for each man with the regular wound dressing MEDS, with stitching needs."

I was, tickled over the fact that she spoke English so well. "Thank you," taking the kit from her. "I like your dress."

Smiling she moved closer, "Ban có thuc su thích nó?"

"In English, please little Missy."

"Do you really like it?" She repeated.

"Yes, I really like it?"

I turned off the lights in the main barracks, leaving the single latrine light in the back of the building on; it gave just enough light to keep it from being totally, dark. I picked her up in my arms and carried her to my bed with her arms wrapped around my neck.

* * * *

"Just proves a man will do anything for pussy, "Layton said after noticing the mirror's hanging on the on exterior of the doors.

I explained. "Maya brought them with her; I didn't go out and buy them."

"Like I said, you're pussy whipped buddy!"

Later in the day, I was, called to the Command Center, Major Baginski and Lt. Higgins was present; I entered with my hat in hand.

"Come in, Sergeant," Baginski said with a wide smile.

I entered, walked right up to his desk, and stood at attention.

"At ease Sergeant, as you were," leaning back in his chair.

"Take a seat," Higgins said taking three cold beers out of the cooler, he gave me one.

The Major popped the top on his beer then took a good long drink. Higgins brought out a bowl of potato chips.

"Have some?"

"No thank you Sir."

"Sergeant, what's your relationship with the Vietnamese nurse under Lt. Hawks command? I do believe, Maya, is that, correct?"

"Yessir, it is. I have a personal relationship with her. She isn't an officer or military," I was worried. "Am I accused of doing anything wrong Sir?"

"Not at all, Sergeant, just the opposite, you are becoming a household name with the civilians around here, whatever you are doing, keep it up."

"I'm confused, Sir."

Finishing his beer, he nodded to Higgins to hand give him another. "Don't be, in fact, we need your input on how to win over the hearts and minds of the Vietnamese people around here," taking a fresh swallow from his new can. "For instance, those mirrors on your barrack doors, they aren't army issue. Tell me what those are all about?"

"Simple Sir, the Vietnamese believe that if a dragon comes to their door, and sees himself in the mirror, the dragon will not attempt to dwell there, because another dragon already resides there."

"Meaning?"

"It's a way to keep the dragon from stealing their spirit, Sir."

"They actually believe this mumbo-jumbo?"

"Just as most American's, believe in, Easter, and Christmas, yessir."

"I'll be damn," turning to Higgins. "Lieutenant, I want you to have supply order mirror's, I want them put on the doors of all of the buildings, this is good stuff."

"The civilian quarters have them already," Higgins offered.

I spoke up. "SGT Savage has his people, I'm sure he could relay to you other traditions which would appeal to them. For instance, there is an Apricot tree which was

129

destroyed when they installed the new M*A*S*H Unit. If you replaced it, I'm sure they would be grateful since that was the only one."

"We have cans of apricots, they are welcome to as many as they want."

"No Sir, cans don't have branches or leafs, the branches are used in the home for decorations during the Tet New Year, they are used to ward off evil spirits."

"I see," Baginski, said turning to Higgins. "Lieutenant, see to it; bring back five or six if you can find them."

Higgins added it to his list.

This went on for a while; we talked, drank beer, and nibbled on chips for more than an hour. Finally, SGT. Savage showed up and took over. I excused myself and got the hell out of there.

1800 came too soon; I had wanted to spend some time with Maya but couldn't. Reyna had the day off, she and Maya had left for Lòng Binh to do some Christmas shopping, later they were going to visit with Maya's mother. Besides, I had to stock my rucksack in preparation for the mission; I had gotten several small plastic bags of rice and some cooked pork roast from the mess hall. Packing them into a smaller bag for sharing with the rest of the team later, done, I applied the camouflage from a burnt cork to my face and the back of my hands. I was finally ready, grabbing my gear I headed for the Huey.

A short time later, we gathered by the Huey with equipment loaded. We were, adorned with our new floppy hats and camouflage uniform; they felt good, a little stiff, but good.

I had my new knife on my right side, wearing the old one on my left side. With a boot, knife in each boot and two eight-inch blades in the middle of my back between the belt and my shirt. I was ready, I felt like a kid at Christmas time. Unlike the Apache, who carried as many as twenty knives, I carried only seven. Because of all of the other gear strapped to my back and sides, that's all I had room for...

In the distance, I spotted Savage talking to a Major from JSOC. Our mission would take us north into the A Shau Valley Region next to Thua Thien Province in I Corps, near the Laotian border.

A Shau Valley being one of the main entry points from North Vietnam to South Vietnam, mainly the Ho Chí Minh Trail. A Shau Valley was critical to North Vietnam. It had long been their supply route for troops, communications, and supplies. The area would remain a target of repeated operations by the U.S. and allied forces. The Viecong and NVA defended it at any cost.

With my K-9 across my back, I stood leaning against a tree checking out the Russian made AK-47. SGT. Savage wanted us to carry the weapon on this mission.

In case we were engaged in a firefight, he wanted us using the same weapons, as the enemy would be employing, all in the hope of confusing Charlie.

I had taped the two banana clips of thirty-rounds of ammo together with the business end facing out on each end. This way I had access to sixty-rounds with one ammo change.

We had a carton of assorted C-rations on the chopper so that when the time came, and depending on what

Commander Shores nutritional needs may be, we were covered. Chances are he or whoever was out there would be dehydrated and hungry.

Savage finishing with the Major joined us at the, Huey, "All right Mates, saddle the fuck, up!"

I sat near the door by the M-60 mounted machine-gun. Our Crew Chief Jewels climbed in after we were aboard; he was short, five-six, possibly five-seven. He's in his late twenties and employed by SGT. Savage for the past six years. Stepping up to the door mounted M-60 he injected a round into the chamber making it ready to fire. Then he snapped the secured line from the floor to the belt around his waist. The line would prevent him from falling out of the helicopter if we encountered any trouble.

The chopper lifted and turned north, we were into a slow, but steady climb. Our altitude finally reached one-thousand-feet where we leveled off. The air speed stopped at ninety-knots. Jewels put his gloves on and took the M-60's grips in hand. His finger on the trigger he shot off a few rounds insuring that the weapon was performing properly.

He wore the gloves because the M-60 often got hot, when fired for an extended period. A canvass bag was attached to it so the shell casings would not fly back hitting the, spinning tail rotor blades. Holes were in the bag with empty C-ration cans. They would aid in the heat disbursal of the spent shell casings.

The pilot, Peaches as everyone called him had been Savage's best friend for the past eleven years. They had described him as a leftover Frenchman from France's occupation here twenty years earlier. I didn't know much about France and Vietnam's relationship. I intended on talking to Peaches about it. Though he was in his late fifties, we would come to find out the man had balls made of steel.

As we flew, Jewels searched the ground looking for any signs of the enemy on the move. He moved the M-60 back and forth wildly the whole time. I thought the guy was kinda nuts. He had this gleam in his eyes as if he were on drugs or something all of the time. He had this endless supply of cherry red suckers. He always had one in his mouth. Long after the candy was gone, he chewed on the white paper sticks until they were mush.

SGT. Tate was our newest addition to the team; he's forty-nine, and a veteran from the Korean War. A decorated Ranger with a stellar combat reputation so we had been told, since he didn't talk about it, we had no idea what a kind of man he actually was, but we were soon to find out.

It wasn't long before we turned into a northwest flight pattern heading straight for the village.

On a road below, Jewels spotted two Vietcong trucks moving beneath us from the northwest.

Peaches had also seen the trucks and started his decent, in an attempt to dodge any gunfire directed our way.

Jewels at the ready, seeking out his targets below, he began blasting away at the trucks. Of course, the Vietcong blasted back, so we joined in and starting firing as well. The AK's projectiles tore through the thin skin of the Huey, but Jewels responded back with dead on accuracy. On fire, the trucks went off the side road crashing into a rock. Holding to the M-60, he screamed, "AMF! AMF!" Translated into (Adios Mother Fuckers!)

Thirty-five minutes later, we were entering the Gates of Hell. Another well-known phrase to describe A Shau Valley; we had finally reached our, LZ (Landing Zone). The Mountain regions in the area provided us with excellent concealment under its green triple-canopied of thick stands of bamboo.

Only problem being, SGT. Savage had described it as so thick that we couldn't get through it. We would have to travel as much as we could under the cover of night. We used a well-traveled road by the North for the final leg of the journey.

Peaches brought the Huey in low and down as quickly as possible! We bailed out at almost the same moment as the chopper came to a momentary stand still! It was floating over the clearing like a giant locust.

Jewels operating the M-60 just in case Charlie was in the area, once on solid ground, we headed for the tree line in the distance. Savage lead the way Layton and I were covering our six.

Peaches punished the Huey by cranking up the RPM's, the blades wrenched under the pressure giving off the usual Whop! Whop! Whop! Pulling itself up, Peaches quickly got outta there by flying low across the valley floor, disappearing into the orange dusk of the setting sun.

We gathered by a large rock where we waited until the Huey was gone, sound and all. SGT. Savage was SL and gave the order to hide the C-rations in the crevasse of the rock. We concealed the containers with leaves. This meant less weight and noise to take with us, which made everyone happy.

Savage led point while Joseph slid into the second slot taking the Slack position. Layton brought up the rear. SGT. Tate was TL. He and I covered our left and right flanks. I kept an eye on our six from time to time.

We moved with weapons at the ready for at least forty-five minutes more before approaching a clearing. SGT. Savage abruptly stopped. Holding his weapon in his right hand, a balled left-handed fist signaled the all stop.

We hunkered down and slowly began filtering into the undergrowth around us. Savage stood like a statue for a long minute before using his left arm bent at the elbow giving us another signal. He was telling us by holding up two crooked fingers that there was a column sized Vietcong column coming our way. Making his fingers loose, he shook his hand back and forth rapidly. A signal we had come up with on our own. Signifying there was too fucking many to count.

In the distance, we heard what Savage had seen. A patrol of Vietcong moving in our direction, it was obvious they hadn't heard the Huey coming or going, or they would have been running with their weapons over their heads screaming orders. These assholes were talking loud speaking of the young girls they had captured from a nearby village. Bragging about what they were going to do them when they got back there, wherever back there was.

Shots of laughter filtered through the column. There were too many to go up against with the pending mission at hand. Probably eighty-to-hundred, or so, we spread out moving deeper into the brush. Realizing the lead section of the column was coming in my direction; I darted behind a clump of small bushes becoming part of the ground as I, was trained to do. Two of the enemy was coming straight at me; I pulled fallen tree branches over me. Using wet leaves and mud, I concealed myself as best I could. I thanked God that it was almost dark. The two men stopped right in front of me, and just inches away. One of them moved to my right. All I could do was hold my breath while I found myself waiting for the worst. Suddenly I was being, sprinkled with urine, but I didn't make a sound. In time, each of them moaned with the joy of relief. Once finished, they walked away talking and laughing among themselves, and finally rejoining the column.

I waited until they were out of earshot, before getting to my feet. By means of some dry leaves, I wiped the liquid off my face.

"Damn, you got pissed on!" Joe laughed.

Layton and Joseph both were quietly laughing their asses off. I on the other hand gave a hand signal all my own, it wasn't a symbol for number one either.

We were only a klick from Hill 936, just a little over three-thousand-feet away. They had planned our insertion to a tee; we wanted to get into place by midnight before making a move on the village. We wanted to approach it on our terms, and so far, we were right on schedule. We started moving again once the column of Vietcong left the area. Using water from my canteen, I washed off the remaining pee I had on my hair and neck.

After a few minutes we stopped at the main road, it would be dark any moment. Making it impossible to see in the dark undergrowth of the bamboo and trees, at this point, we took the Green Eye (Starlight Night Vision) scope from our packs before moving on.

Then, forced to stop again while taking shelter in the trees; we spotted a line of enemy trucks coming toward us in the distance. However, this road led right to the village where the Commander was being, held.

We had no choice but to wait for the trucks to pass. Being dark the light from their headlights were screwing with our night vision. I sat with my eyes closed, which wasn't good either. However, on the up side, it didn't take as long for my eyes to refocus. In ten minutes or less, we were up moving again, we walked at a fast pace letting the moon light lead our way, and we would still bring the scopes up peering through them at different intervals. Making sure that the area around us were absent of any would be hostile's. Twenty-minutes later, we found ourselves closing to within five-hundred yards of the suspected village. Savage gave the order to stop again. We spread the team out putting twenty-foot between us. While bending over at the waist, we moved with weapons at the ready while entering the south end of the village. The moon casting shadows through the trees overhead as we followed a well-worn path toward our objective. Staying in the shadows, we moved quietly and cautiously. We were so deep within enemy territory we weren't concerned with booby-traps. Closing in, we stopped fifty-feet away. Everyone noticing the absence of sounds, it was quiet, unusually quiet.

It's then we heard them, two men in the distance were arguing over a plate of food. We inched closer and listened in on their conversation. They were standing in front of a small building nearest to us. One man wanted to feed the American, while the other one wanted the food for himself. While the other yelling, and complaining that their captain wanted to keep the American alive.

Savage turned signaling to us to recon our way around the remaining two buildings in the compound. The two men had their attention on each other and not us. It was plain to see that the, two buildings were occupied; we could see shadowy figures moving by the windows of both of them. Tate and Joseph went to check the first building, while Layton and I were to take the remaining smaller structure. We waited for Joseph and Tate to reach their objective first. Tate signaled that they were ready giving a hand signal saying they were four Vietcong inside. We signaled the ok as we started toward our target. Once there we peered through the open windows of the edifice. Inside we saw six children bound and gagged setting in a corner. Two Vietcong were taking turns raping a fourteen-year-old girl. They had her tied spread eagle on a metal bunk bed. I raised the K-9 into firing position while Layton moved to the other opened window in case I missed. With careful aim, I pumped two silent rounds into the back of the head of the asshole awaiting his turn. He dropped to the floor like the turd he was. The man on top of the girl jumped to his feet. During his attempt to pull his trousers up, I pumped four rounds into his chest, he went down. Covering the front door, Layton went inside, giving the '*all clear*', I followed. We decided to leave the young girl and the children as they were for the moment. Protocol required clearing and securing the rest of the compound first. The two men in front of the first hooch were still arguing over the food.

Tate and Joseph had cleared the second house. At this point, all of us had passed to within ten-feet of the two men shouting at each other. Neither of them had any idea that we were there. Savage had checked out the small building. Signaling that Commander Shore may be in there or at least someone, he believed to be an American.

Joseph and Tate were in position. When Savage gave the order, Tate walked up behind the man with the plate, while Joseph approached the other. The man wanting the plate of food for himself, slapped the plate out of the other man's hands. It was at the same moment, Tate and Joseph grabbed them in unison from behind putting a well-placed blade into their rib cages. Both men were dead by the time they hit the ground.

Layton and I were at the front porch of the building in only seconds. Peering through the window, I saw a man tied to a wooden chair with a straw seat. He looked American. He sat slumped over. His restraints were the only thing keeping him upright in the chair. His wrists were bloody and bound behind him. His hair was a bloody mess, and his scalp was missing hair in spots. As if, they pulled it out of his head by the handful. I could only see him from the back. He was nude from the waist up and shoeless. His back supported heavy bruising and deep lash marks. Dried blood spotted his back and shoulder blades. Layton inspected for any signs of booby-traps before opening the door. Tate had taken the pajama top off one of the dead Vietcong bringing into the hooch with him. Layton cut away the small ropes freeing the Commander. His fingers were missing at the first joints on each hand, but they had left his thumbs intact. The area around his mouth was badly scared from having his teeth knocked out with a blunt object, probably with a rifle butt. He's semiconscious. Tate handed me the sandals he had taken from the enemy.

The sandals wouldn't stay on his feet; then I realized they had cut off all of his toes. We pulled the blacktop over his head straightening it out over his upper body. I injected him with Morphine to relax him. He would most likely experience some form of euphoria as a reaction, or at least I hoped so. Layton lifted the Commander up laying him across his shoulder. At that point, we went back outside. Tate and Joseph staying behind dragging the two dead Vietcong inside the hooch, Outside Layton handed the Commander off to SGT. Savage with Joseph's help.

"We have nine children and a young girl in the hooch we cleared," I said in a low voice. "What do you want us to do?"

"Bring them," Savage said, as he and Joseph left with the Commander.

Together, Layton, Tate and I headed for the shack. Inside the children were terrified. We must have looked like boogey man with our faces blacken and mud everywhere with guns in our hands. We cut the ropes from the young girl first who had been tied to the bed sitting her free. She was bleeding from her vagina; the skin around it had been, badly damaged. I applied ointment to her wounds while Tate applied a small bandage to her upper thigh.

"Chúng tôi đang o đây đe giúp ban. Chúng tôi không làm ton thuong ban goikng." (We are here to help you. We are not going to hurt you). Trying to calm her down as the others worked freeing the younger children.

I decided to inject her with a shot of Morphine only because of her pain, in minutes she had calmed down enough to talk calmly.

"Ho đã giet me và cha tôi." (They killed my mother and father).

"Nó là ok sweetie, Đó là, hãy nói cho tre nho, chúng tôi đang o đây đe đua ho đen an toàn (It is ok sweetie, please tell the younger children we are here to take them to safety.). Hoping to calm them down. Coming from the older girl would be better than coming from us.

She was weak but she moved toward them saying. "Chúng tôi là an toàn bây gio, hãy cho chúng tôi voi vàng." (We are safe now let us hurry).

Ready, we headed for the extraction point. We took turns carrying the girl as well as the one-year-old. The girl was just too weak from not eating and being, abused. She was far too delicate to walk on her own.

Having plenty of time, we stopped allowing the children to rest several times along the way. We used the Green Eye to make sure the area was safe before moving out. Layton and I had cooked rice in our packs; we gave it to the girl and baby. The full moon had turned out to be a blessing. It had made travel a lot easier. It was as if God Himself had ordained this rescue.

Twenty-minutes later, we reached the rest of the group. Hearing us approaching they used the scopes to make sure that it was us. Upon reaching the others, we began opening the C-rations making them ready for the children.

Starved and weak, we fed Commander Shore soft foods being careful to stay away from sugars. Having an assortment to choose from, we gave him mashed potatoes, and beefsteak gravy. Turned out to be the best since he didn't have any teeth.

There were also beans with soft wieners. He ate slowly managing to keep it down. Once done eating we made him comfortable and let him sleep.

The sun began breaking on the horizon. The first shots of sunlight were cresting over the mountains in the distance. The scene was as beautiful as a child's smile.

Knowing Charlie would be listening to all radio communication. Savage used the 'Break Squelch' method to communicate with us. Peaches pressed the talk button once making a hissing noise on our end. No voices were, heard. Making it impossible for our location to be, detected, Savage pressed the talk button five times, each with five long hisses lasting three seconds each. Signaling that it's safe for him to come in. We received three hisses in return, which told us that he was on his way. If all went as expected, he and Jewels would be here within fifteen minutes or less. We spread out moving to the cover of the bush where we waited.

Joseph moved in from the west pointing back to where he had been standing watch. In the distance, two large trucks were moving our way; the first truck had an M-60 attached to a fixed tripod on the bed of the truck. A single driver with three in the back of the vehicle, the second truck was larger and armed with quad 50's. An anti-aircraft weapon left over from WWII. There were three in the front seat and two in the back with the massive gun.

The quad 50 was made up of four electric solenoid-fired 50 Cal machine-guns mounted on to a movable turret, mounted to a truck similar to our 2 ½ ton.

We were thinking they were on routine patrol since they were in no particular hurry. Across the field were large rocks with a ravine next to an insignificant stand of trees near a small stream.

"What now?" Joseph asked.

Savage, flustered. "No worries, Mate, I'll just run down there and stab' em all too bloody death." Keying up the radio, he sent the SOS to Peaches by way of several more clicks telling him to stand down.

Tate chiming in. "They are relaxed; let's let them get settled in. It's early, maybe they haven't had breakfast yet."

We settled back down for the wait, after a few minutes, they had backed the trucks in under the cover of the trees, and then turned off the engines. Two went to the creek for water, while some others gathered food from the cabs of the trucks. One man moved to the base of the rocks taking the high ground standing guard.

Tate moved in keeping low. "I'll take, Logan and Sacks in from this side. We can get to them without their knowing, take'em out one by one, and clean."

Savage looked at me, referring to my K-9. "Can you take them out with that P'shooter at a distance?"

"Dead on at eighty-feet."

Savage looking at Tate, "Do it, Layton, and I will take the left?"

Hunkered over, we scattered out moving through the high grass toward the trucks. We put thirty-feet between the three of us moving quietly but as fast as possible. In less than twenty-minutes, we had closed to within hundred-feet of their location. From there, we lost sight of each other as we went deeper into the brush.

I headed for the guard at the rocks; SGT. Tate with Joseph at his side went for the main body of men. Once at the rocks, I saw SGT. Tate forty-feet away. The Vietcong were sitting in a circle eating and talking. One bitched about his tea being too hot to drink. From where they were sitting, they could see the guard, if I took him out now, they would surely know. Then one of them got up and began walking toward the creek for more water. Joseph was waiting there like a trap-door spider. When Chuck was out of sight from the rest of his men, Joseph took him out with his knife.

The guard looked in my direction but then turned back around. A comrade called out to him telling him to come get something to eat while yet another man walked toward the rock to take his place. I faded back into the brush where I waited until the guard climbed down and left.

His replacement moved to the front of the rock, doing so placed the man out of view of the others and in my line of fire. Holding a cup of tea in one hand, he went about the business of relieving himself with the other. I quietly walked up behind him reaching for his chin grabbing the back of his head at the same time; I gave it a quick violent twist, snapping his neck. Holding onto his limp body, I gently laid him on the ground front of me so he wouldn't make any noise.

Moving back to the left side of the rock, I saw Tate moving up to another man sitting right in front of him on a log, with his back to Tate. The little man is enjoying a home rolled cigarette while busy retying his bootlace. With no one to see, Tate snatched the small man off the log dragging him into the brush. By the time the enemy soldier hit the ground, he was dead.

Joseph was on the move, working his way into position on the other side.

Two more men were at the front of the first truck and out of view of the others. I knew I could hit both men with the K-9 from here, but the headshots had to be dead on. I clicked off the safety then waited for SGT. Tate to get in position to attack again, once he was ready; I raised my weapon firing two rounds hitting my mark. The second man shocked, looked right at me, I dropped him in the same manner before he was able to react. Tate and Joseph took down two others. We had got in clean, now all we had to do was get out clean. Myself, and Tate wired C-4 to the Quad 50's while Joseph went to Savage asking him to call Peaches for an extraction. We had to destroy the Quad 50's that was from an unknown overran Marine Fire Base at one point. I unlocked the M-60 taking it with us. All after connecting the Det Cord to the C4, giving us approximately twenty-minutes to make our getaway...

"Good work, men," Savage said. "It was all over by the time Layton and I got into place."

In the distance, we heard the familiar sounds of the Huey's blades slicing through the morning air. It's well-passed dawn, in fact, it's almost eleven, quiet time was over, we had to get everyone on board and get the hell outta there.

Peaches sat the Huey down a few yards away, the grass twisting and curling in all directions from the heavy prop wash.

Jewels operated the M-60 securing the area as we loaded. I handed him the other M-60 from the truck, he smiled like a bird fed cat. "Thank you, buddy!"

We loaded the Commander first, then the injured girl and the younger child. The kids were next, we followed once they were aboard and seated. We held to the children respectfully as we made ready for takeoff. Peaches got us in the air, and headed for home. A short time later, the C-4 exploded into a large red ball of fire, igniting the gasoline in the trucks.

Marine Sniper Charles Whitman
kills 16 people at the University of Texas
08/01/66
Comedian Lenny Bruce dies
of a drugs overdose
08/03/66
Stars & Stripes

CHAPTER NINE

BASE CAMP: Peaches brought the chopper in quickly sitting it down on the landing pad near the M*A*S*H Unit. Dust, leaves, and debris were twisting, and blowing in the violent wind made by the whooping blades. Once down, Savage stepped down from the chopper and headed for the Command Post. Peaches cut the engine.

The medical staff with, others were standing by to remove Commander Shore and the young girl from the chopper first. The rest of us helped with the remaining children. I carried the one-year-old while Tate, Layton, and Joseph helped with the others.

Slowly the spinning blades had come to a stop. While Peaches secured the blade to the rotor secti1on to keep it from being, caught in the wind. Jewels made sure that everyone got out without tripping or falling. With the baby in my arms, we entered the hospital with all of the children. The nurses came to help us. One by one, they took the children to an examination room. I followed them with the baby who was badly dehydrated, pale, weak, and unresponsive. Maya came into the room, and seeing the baby's condition she took the child from my arms.

"Tôi muon đua anh ay đen bác si ngay lap tuc Finch!" (I want to take him to Doctor Finch right away).

Layton and I walked back out into the hallway.

Reyna came out of an operating room at the end of the hall, seeing us she yelled out, "Jack!"

Layton and I stopped in our tracks and waited for her.

"Can you tell me how the older girl was injured? We are having problems stopping the bleeding."

Wasn't an easy way to say it, so I just said it, "She was a virgin, so one of the assholes that raped her opened her up with broom handle?"

"Good God!" She grimaced looking at me, "What about the baby you brought in, is the mother here?"

"The girl and the baby are sisters; the bastards killed their mother, and father along with the elders when they raided their village."

"The other children?"

"No relation as far as I know," I related.

* * * *

Two hours later, we were, we finally had the time to take a shower and eat chow. It felt good to be clean again; all that we needed now were a few hours of sleep.

While at the mess hall, Maya stepped in joining Layton and me at our table. She brought extra chocolate milk and gave it to me.

"Thank you," as she sat down.

"You're welcome," she smiled.

Joseph trailed in bringing his tray to the table sitting next to Layton, while nodding in Maya's direction. "Hi there," he said.

"Hi Joseph," she answered.

We laughed at the way she pronounced his name.

"You laugh at me," looking at us in turn.

"Not at all," Layton said.

"I not know about that."

Diverting her attention, "What about the other kids, are they going to be ok?" I asked.

"They are weak, but doctor say they will be ok; the people here are taking in the kids as their own. Even the older girl and her baby sister has, been spoken for. They have no other place to go."

"Good," we all agreed.

Maya looked at me with affection. "You looked very good holding the baby. You make good father one day," she said.

Being, teased by the others, "Maybe someday." I said.

"Yes, someday," she added.

By 1800 Layton and I had turned in, it had been a long day we were bone tired.

Maya is working the night shift, so I would meet her for breakfast and plan for our Christmas Eve party tomorrow night. She wanted to have Layton meet a new nurse who arrived while we were, gone. Maya says she's shy, but very pretty. According to Maya, she wants to meet an American GI. Maybe it was the way she said it. I got the impression her girlfriend wanted, to get married to an American and go stateside no matter who he was.

I was up early, around five, so I got the three 'S' out of the way and brushed my teeth. Layton was still sawing logs; Joseph was nowhere to be, found. I figured he had a more eventful night than I did.

I sat dressed only in boxer shorts looking out of the window next to me. The morning was soft and quiet like Maya looks when she was sleeping. Morning clouds floated against the beauty of the rising sun. It's hard to believe this place as beautiful as it is can be so deadly at the same time.

Layton rolled to the edge of his bed and sat straight up. Rubbing the sleep out of his eyes, "What are you doing?"

"Thinking."

"Oh, working without tools again are we?"

"Hey!"

"Joe must have gotten lucky," he said on the way to the bathroom.

"You are in a good mood for a change. What kind of dream did you have?"

Yelling from the shower, "I don't dream anymore! Not since I've been here anyway!"

While he got a shower, I made notes in my journal about what had transpired in the field yesterday and how I felt especially sorry for the girl who was, raped.

She's probably in for a rough time. Her future filled with difficulty when it comes to dealing with men.

Experiencing the inhumanity to man first hand. Has caused me to question my belief in God, God and my belief in Him constructed the foundation of which I am, or becoming. I am changing. That scares me. I am, liking what I do. To take another's life under the influence of adrenaline, no matter how vile that life may have been. Has tarnished my soul, and not in a bad way. The experience has empowered me. It is becoming easier and easier to simply extinguish the living soul. The Bible says in Genesis that God created man, a living soul. The military praises us for killing them, offering medals and awards for doing the deed. There are wars and people dying throughout the Old Testament. Example after example of the prophets doing God's biddings, as my young mind explained it away. God sanctifies actions of the military machine. So why fight it I argued with myself. After all, the South Vietnamese was being killed and oppressed. All they were asking was to help them overcome the enemy from the north, and we were here to do just that.

It's eight o'clock and the mess hall is full of people. The walls were, covered with reds and green decorations. The tables were, covered with tablecloths of that same red and greens. Peaches brought a Christmas tree in from Saigon; the villagers decorated it with more reds and greens via SGT. Savage's directions. There was a stack of presents under the tree for everyone.

The Vietnamese in the compound didn't understand the concept of Christmas, regardless; they were having a good time. Sharing the gifts with the newly arrived children turned out to be the highlight of the evening. Everyone was laughing, talking, drinking, eating, and passing out gifts.

Layton, Joseph, and I were tearing off pieces of meat from the turkey in front of us and washing it down with beer. Maya sat across from me imitating us eating like the barbarians we pretending to be.

"This is much fun," she yelled with a turkey leg in her hand, then taking a delicate bite, "Mmm, this taste good!"

The Major and Higgins were at the officer's table with Reyna. She looked especially beautiful tonight. It was the first time I had seen her in civilian clothes in at least four years. Her figure did wonders for the Ao Dai she was wearing. Her dark brown hair hung with curls across her shoulders and down her back.

"She very much pretty," Maya said coming to my side.

I turned to her. "Yes she is. Did you get her that dress?"

"Mother, pick it for her, all three of us went shopping together on Tuesday. Mother, make it, Christmas present, nice. No?"

"Nice, yes?"

Save Your Heart for Me, by Gary Lewis and the Playboys was playing on the record player. Savage served as our DJ for the night.

As I got to my feet, I reached for her hand, "Dance with me you chocolate eyed beauty."

"I not sure how, "displaying her usual smile.

Once on the dance floor, I told her to put her feet on top of mine. She laughed and sniggered as we moved across the floor. "Oh this much fun, "she giggled.

We kept this up until the song ended, and then we headed back to the table.

Joseph had replaced the empty beer bottles with new ones, and then asked Maya to dance with him. They left for the dance floor as *'What's New Pussycat' by Tom Jones* started. Maya laughed at Joseph's antics as he tried teaching her to dance.

"What about me?" Reyna said stopping at our table.

Our gaze meeting, "You wanna dance?"

"Sure, why not? Holding out her hand, as I stood placing a hand at the small of her back, taking her to the dance floor, "I'm not into Tom Jones. Care if we wait for the next one?"

"Not at all," she said. "Maya looks sexy tonight."

"Yes, she does, for that matter, so do you."

She nodded, "Thank you kind sir," with a smile. "The last time we were on the dance floor together. You were mad at me. Remember?"

"I do. That was the night I let you go, God that was a lifetime ago."

"You broke up with me, you didn't let me go." Removing a small box from a pocket, she handed it to me, "I hope you don't mind, I got you a little something."

"How sweet of you, thank you very much," I sighed. "And no, I let you go, "opening the box. "It's a wristwatch," I said surprised.

"What's the difference from breaking up and letting me go?"

"I let you go to see if you would come back after me, you didn't. That told me that I didn't mean anything to you."

"Oh Jack, you have no idea what I was going through at the time. You worked on the farm seven-days a week and our time was so limited. I thought you didn't want to bother with me anymore. You broke my heart. I had to let you leave."

"I guess one excuse is better than any other."

"Let's not fight," she smiled. Then back to the watch, "I figured with your line of work, you wouldn't want a brass or silver one?"

"No, this is great, thank you." I said, putting it on. It was all black with a compass in the center of it. "It fits too."

Unchained Melody by the Righteous Brothers began.

Reaching for her, "Shall we?"

"We shall," she said moving in close.

"I got you, a little something as well," sliding my hand around her waist.

"Oh?" She said looking into my eyes.

"I was going to bring it to you later, but now will do. It will save me a trip," waiting to get a slap for being so indifferent.

After a short pause, "Where is it?"

I removed my arm from her back, then retrieved the dark blue long velvet case from my pocket, and gave it to her.

"Oh Jack, you shouldn't have," she said removing a gold necklace from the box. "Oh this is beautiful," stepping back turning around for me to put it on her. She held her hair off her shoulders while I placed it around her neck. She embraced the pearl at the bottom of the chain with her right hand. "How does it look?"

"On you, it's beautiful." I fought the urge of taking her face into my palms pulling her lips into mine. I wanted to kiss her deeply and take her out of here.

She kissed me on the cheek. "Thank you Jack, I will never take it off."

Regaining my composure, "You can tell Charles its payment for you attending to me while I was laid up in the hospital. Maybe he won't get jealous?"

"There isn't any Charles," she said peering at me.

My face had to show my confusion, or at least my surprise! "What's that supposed to mean?"

Once the song ended, we returned to the others seated at the table, "We need to talk." kissing me on the mouth this time before walking away.

"Damn bro you look like you are suffering from shell-shock. What happened?" Layton, muttered.

I sat down, Maya had gone to the bathroom, and Joseph was getting more beer. "Women!" I finally managed to say.

Maya coming to the table with her friend,

"Sergeant Layton, this is Chau, my friend."

Layton and I stood up. "Nice to meet you;" he smiled with me following with a nod.

"Also nice to meet you," Chau replied.

Layton slid back the chair for her to sit. Once she sat down, we took our seats. She was very pretty; I couldn't help thinking that she looked a lot like Nancy Kwan the movie star.

Maya caught my attention by handing me large box wrapped in bright red Christmas paper. It had a large yellow ribbon on it. I opened it, to my surprise; I found a stereo reel-to-reel tape recorder with matching speakers. My face lit up.

"You like?"

I kissed her, "I, like very much," I sighed grinning from ear to ear.

Joseph returned with more beer, he was getting loopy. "Man, I think I need to go lay down."

"You do seem out of it my friend."

"I am more tired than drunk; I haven't had any sleep for almost three days."

"Why don't you take off get some rest?"

Holding to his stomach, "I think I will," getting up and walking away looking as if he had to puke.

Everyone said his or her goodbyes to him along with Christmas wishes as he left.

Maya and I excused us leaving Layton and Chau alone to be better acquainted.

We left straight for the supply room since Joe would be back at the, barracks. I intended on bringing her here anyway. The place was empty this time of night, there was a lock on the door, and I unlocked it. Switched on a single overhead light and locked the door behind us from the inside.

"You think SGT. Layton like my friend?"

"Yes, she's very pretty, looks like Nancy Kwan," I said.

"Who is Nancy Kwan?"

"A movie star back home."

"Do I look like Nancy Kwan?"

"No, you are more beautiful than Nancy Kwan!"

"What is movie star?" She played.

"You've never seen a movie?"

"No."

"Do you have a TV?"

"No."

"We'll have to fix that. As soon as I can, I'm taking you to a movie."

"See Nancy Kwan?"

Laughing, "If we can, yes."

I had put her presents behind the counter earlier. Holding to her tiny waist, I sat her up on the counter in front of me. "Wait right here," giving her a quick kiss. Gone but a minute I returned with three small boxes. She was as excited as a child would be. Her eyes were bright and her smile was perfect.

"For me?"

"Yes Missy for you."

Opening the first box, she found her favorite perfume, "I excited, very nice!" She giggled. Opening the second box containing sexy silk undergarments, "Ahh these for you," she said taking the lid off.

"Yeah, but they pull the hair under my arms."

She laughed, picking up the last box. She removed a small gold strand mother of pearl necklace, "Ohhh this," with big wide eyes. "This is most beautiful," she said, holding it in her hand. "When I small girl my grandmother gave me same one."

"I can take it back."

"On no, it is good luck you get same one, it means grandmother approves of you! I am very blessed," putting it on.

"I am glad that you like it."

"Jack?" As I moved between her legs, nestling in closer to her while using her hips to pull her forward. "You make love to me gently now?"

"We don't have to do this. Are you sure you want to?"

"Yes please," she smile. "I want very much."

"Then yes, I make love to you gently now."

*So long as you are secure, you will
count many friends; if your life becomes
clouded, you will be alone.
Ovid (43 BC-18 AD)*

Chapter Ten

THE VALLEY OF TEARS: Looking back I can say that my life has definitely become cloudy. I was no longer the naïve farm boy I was when I joined the Army in what seems so many years ago.

My conscience was killing me. All the while, I was making love to Maya last night; all I could think about was Reyna. I was being an ass to her because I felt that she was playing more games with me. I wasn't exactly sure what was happening, but I liked the kiss Reyna gave and wondered what her remark about Charles meant. I fell like an ass by taking Mayas virginity. I've wished a thousand times it never happened, but it did. No matter, it will have to wait.

The CQ (Charge of Quarters) awakened Layton and me at 1800.

We had received an emergency mission order. Layton was already in the latrine brushing his teeth when I found him. We both were usually grouchy when first awaken; though it was six in the evening, neither of us had gone to bed until after two this afternoon. He had been with Chau while I dropped Maya off at her mother's in Long Binh before returning to camp. To save comments we may later regret neither of us spoke.

I was truly tired of brushing my teeth with no toothpaste, but the dangers were just too great to start now. Besides any smells out there could mean the difference between life and death. Therefore, we did what we had to do and went for supper.

The mess hall was crowded, however we found two seats in the rear near the kitchen.

"How did it go with you and, Chau last night?" Finally thinking of something to say that might not piss him off, as I dug into mashed potatoes.

"She's a keeper I think, very nice."

"Her name, Chau, it means, pearls, or precious stones."

He looked at me. "You always do that!"

"Do what?"

"Tell me what shit means." Thinking, he then came out with, "Since she's so small, I suppose I could call her, Minnie Pearl!"

I laughed, "I doubt that."

"Me to," he grinned.

* * * *

MISSION: MA9421 LRRP Hau Bon Province II Corps, Water Insertion:

Forty-minutes later, we were flying North West just a few feet above the jungle canopy. The countryside is beautiful, the lush valleys, the green grass of the wide-open spaces. The surface of the lakes glimmered like millions of small diamonds in the sun. I would like to stay up here for the rest of time just to take it all in.

Nevertheless, reality was reality; both of us began the dutiful task of checking our equipment and weapons. We were carrying the SwedishK-9 accompanied with two C4 blocks each, hand grenades and so forth.

We had the two single air tanks lying down on their sides; we had them tied to the floor to prevent them from falling over and damaging the valves and regulators. Having our scuba masks around our necks, we wore our uniforms instead of the wet suit. It was hot and dry. We figured that the uniforms would dry in no time. Our socks boots and other supplies stuffed into waterproof bags for easier carrying.

I stuffed the PRC-25 radio nicknamed the, (PRICK because of cumbersome carrying and use) into a separate waterproof bag. Normally we carried the PRC-77: radio, similar to PRC-25, it had an encryption device for making secure communications. On this mission though, it didn't matter if Charlie overheard our conservation or not. For we hoped he would never be able to figure out what we were talking about until it was too late to do anything about it.

Putting on our flippers, the pilot gave the two-minute warning to Water Drop. We were ready, Layton on the left side of the chopper, me on the right.

We had drawn a pilot, Warrant Officer Johnson from the 1st Cav. I would have felt better if Peaches had been at the helm, but no one had much control over the situation when it comes directly from JSOC.

Air tanks on our back, gear secured to our bodies. We waited for the drop command. The chopper dipped down toward the lake once we had cleared the last of the foliage. Thirty-feet, twenty, and then eight-feet off the top of the water, the pilot reduced his air speed to ten-knots. We were entering the water low, and finally Johnson gave the signal. We dropped butt first knowing the chopper's noise would cover the splash of the impact. Johnson gunned the Huey and in a flash; he was gone, its sounds dying in the distance. The late evening brought in dampness, the lake had developed a late evening gray fog over it. Floating three-feet high off the surface of the, water, we drifted for a few minutes listening for any signs that Charlie may have spotted the Huey. Using the fog as concealment, we stayed at the surface as we made our way toward shore. Pushing ourselves along silently through the water with our flippers, there was no reason to submerge, so we turned off our air valves to our tanks since we no longer needed them. We swam the distance using the fog to our advantage. Within twenty-minutes, we were over half way to the riverbank. Closing in, we could see the treetops and the tree line of the jungle where it intermixed with a stand of large trees. A small white sandy beach came in to view.

Without incident, and minutes later, we had reached land. Moving to some large overhanging bushes located in a thicket of trees. We carefully searched the ground in front of us for any would be booby-traps, and personnel mines. Once at the large shrubs, we stopped and dropped down on both knees.

The birds were singing as they looked down at us from their lofty perch's. The monkeys in the trees chattered and barked as they scurried about. We got out our dry socks and jungle boots and put them on. Then hurriedly we retrieved our gear from the plastic bags.

I had never seen so many dragonflies so large, they looked like small helicopters, it was clear that the evenings' insects were beginning to make themselves known. We stored the air tanks inside the large tree like bush.

Layton would carry the radio for the first leg of the journey; I would carry it on the way back.

According to our map, there was an old abandon mine field which lay just to the south of us, maybe a hundred-feet or so from our present position. Intel had received reports of Vietcong and arms massing just two miles on the other side of the hill in front of us. Mines and booby-traps, littered the lakeshore. We came in above them. Whoever planned our insertion had good Intel.

I thought of Maya as we headed out, I was sure Layton was thinking of Chau, or someone. I had no idea since he wasn't one to express his thoughts or feelings about much of anything. If Andy wanted you to know something, he would tell you, and he seldom answered a personal question, so I had long since stopped asking.

We nodded to each other as we began moving. I took point since he carried the radio, if the point man had the radio and was hit; chances are we would lose the radio leaving the other man stranded.

If the map was correct, we should come out on the upper end of the old mine field and be in no danger, if not; so be it. We had to look carefully at our surroundings, especially the ground. Many things in the jungle can kill you and all of them are nasty.

It's getting dark now, which put pressure on us to find a secure spot to spend the night. About fifty-feet away, we spotted a small escarpment, which would provide shelter. Inching our way along, we finally made our way up to its base taking a seat near an opening in the rocks. Retrieving our Green Eye's, we began searching the area around us, but it wasn't dark enough to see well, so we would have to wait until it got a little darker.

While waiting, I spotted a snake going up a small tree beside me about five-feet in length. Its head and neck is uncolored, with rounded spots joined along the length of its body blending in as it tapered out. It was a *'Beauty Rat Snake'*.

Leaning in, I snatched it up holding to its head. Using both hands, I twisted its head off its body. The dying snake thrashed about in the dirt and the dry leafs making a lot of noise. I picked up a nearby log from, a fallen tree and placed it down across its body; the weight of the log stopped it from thrashing about.

After a time, "Clear," Layton whispered putting away the night scope, "There's nothing out there."

I took a bar of C4 from my pack and using my K-bar I cut a quarter of it into small chucks.

Layton cleaned away a small space between us finding a few small flat surfaced rocks, and sat about making a base for cooking.

The C4 is excellent for preparing meals; its smokeless, odorless and a sure-heat-source. I lit one of the chunks with a match then laid it on the rock bed. Then went about slicing our dinner into three-inch oblong pieces, removing the snake's skin was a chore, but I got it done after cleaning out the entrails. We stuck the chunks of meat on two-small sticks that Layton had gleaned from the forest. The scene made me think of toasting, marshmallows. In like manner, we cooked the snake.

In there somewhere, we wished each other a Merry Christmas. Layton took the first watch, and every few minutes he used the night vision scope to survey the area. We secretly hoped the Vietcong didn't have the same technology as we had. Command knew China was working on the science of night vision, but we guessed the NVA would have it before the Vietcong would.

If not for the mines and booby-traps in the area, we could have moved further inland during the night, but not knowing where they were, we were forced to wait for daylight. I was a wake by 0100, so I relieved Layton of guard duty and let him get some sleep.

I took a large portion of the snake with me for a late snack, with the exception of the bones, the meat tasted like fresh water perch.

A couple of hours passed before I began looking around with the Starlight, I spotted a deer a few meters away. Deer in Vietnam only grow to the size of a large dog; I remember thinking that he would have made a great Christmas Dinner.

It was now breaking dawn; I took out the few chocolate bars we had brought with us. The slang name for them was *John Wayne Bars*. You had to be John Wayne in order to eat the damn things. The candy would serve a twofold purpose; the sugars would give us energy thereby killing our appetite at the same time. However, we would eat them later; daylight wasn't something to be wasted.

With long sticks in hand, we probed the ground in front of us as we made our way through the scrub. Finally, we came to a wide path cleared by the Vietcong, so we stopped. Layton found a freshly planted land mine I had overlooked. I wasn't scared, but I got scared after I had time to think about it. Beyond me lay another one, then another. I carefully backtracked to his position. In front of him there was a string leading to the trunk of a small tree. At its base, two sticks making an arrow pointed to where the mine was, placed. The path in front of us was well worn; it appeared that a great deal of foot traffic had come through here as recently as yesterday. This meant only one thing, the people who planted the mines had marked them so their comrades would have safe passage. We had to make sure this didn't happen. Beating them to the punch as it were, Layton and I sat about removing all of the markers as we continued moving forward concealing the mines from the enemy. This process lasted for sixty-meters or more, taking almost two-hours to complete.

Once we were done, we stepped out of the wooded area and entered the mouth of a large clearing. The grass in front of us had been pushed flat just as the path we had just left.

Putting the compass and the map together, we knew we were getting closer. Chances were we wouldn't find any more mines in this area; they had only been interested in mining the obvious passages. Once we had completed the mission, we would have to return to this point on the way back. From here, we would have to travel due west until we reached the river. Then we would move down to the lake from there.

An hour later, we came to another tree line; we heard faint voices in the distance. Layton stayed behind while I investigated. Lying flat on my stomach, I moved to an observation point. The suns in my face meaning that I couldn't use my binoculars. The glare reflecting off one of the lens could mean certain death, a sniper's climax come true. We had found it; I motioned to Layton, and slowly moved farther down the ridge and out of sight.

The Vietcong in the valley below numbered at least six-hundred strong. It was obvious that their camp had been here for a while. Laundry on clotheslines, litter everywhere, latrine ditches dug, an ammo dump sat just south of what looked like a mess hall. There were approximately thirty-four large trucks, with a fuel depot setting at the south end.

Using my Sextant, I worked out the longitude and the latitude and wrote it down. It appeared that some trucks were getting ready to move out. I could make out eleven-trucks that had already been loaded, the drivers of those trucks seem to be just standing around waiting on the others to finish.

Almost forty-minutes had passed; I had to recheck my information to insure everything was correct, mainly the information and logistics of the area. Command would later use the gathered facts I had listed including the strike results, thereby studying their effectiveness. Completed, now was the time to make haste. We had to get back across the clearing to safety.

We double-timed our way back, stopping only twice to catch our breath. Once we had returned to the edge of the clearing, we stopped flopping down near a large thicket. The minefield was only feet away.

I fired up the PRICK. Since Charlie can hear our transmission, we used some predetermined chatter we thought might confuse the ole boys, I began.

Into the Radio, "This is The Pancake Man. Is The Pan Ready? – Over," nothing but long 'hisses', "I repeat, This Is The Pancake Man, Is The Pan Ready? - Over."

Back at us, "The Pan Is Ready, Where's The Pancake Mix? – Over."

I read off the numbers, "Latitude 12.48333-34 Longitude 109.06667-46" On both sides we knew the minus 34 and 46 meant nothing. We hoped that by the time Chuck figured it out, it would be too late.

"Roger - Over and Out," the radio conversation ended abruptly.

The message had keyed artillery strikes from twenty-five miles away, the Plojo's; (Two-Hundred-Pound Artillery Shells) were on the way. Fighter jets with bombs and napalm to hit soon, after.

We didn't stick around for the air show, our mission was complete, and we were up and moving toward the water, with the radio over my shoulder.

Just then from behind us in the jungle, we heard mines exploding and Vietcong screaming along the path that we had prepared for them; the Vietcong had managed to trigger at least three of the mines before stopping. Chances are they had no idea we were even in the area. The mines would keep them at bay while we made our escape.

Ten-minutes later, we were at the edge of a cliff overlooking the lake below. The water is at least thirty-feet below us, and it's too shallow to dive. We would have to make our way further down the ridge to reach freedom.

Deciding to move into the edge of the jungle, we stayed at the top edge of the cliff as much as possible when we moved.

Layton was in the lead, I stayed ten-feet behind with the radio. While moving we heard the explosions taking place in the distant valley.

Unexpectedly, I heard a low growl, but even so, it was loud. "What the fuck was that!" I stammered.

In a blink of an eye a five-hundred pound eight-foot long Indochinese Tiger came out of nowhere attacking Layton knocking him to the ground!

My training covering animal attacks flashed through my mind like a bolt of lightning! *'They are the largest of all cats,' o*ur instructors warned us. *'They are capable of covering a span of thirty-yards a second once at full speed. They can jump over an elephants head or a height of sixteen-feet from a dead stand still.'*

The Tiger's massive claws ripped into Layton's body! Layton was squirming, kicking, and fighting for his life with everything he had! The Tiger's large mouth opened, and his knife like teeth sank into Layton's neck biting all the way through!

Layton's body went limp! All of this happening in just a matter of seconds! The Tigers massive teeth tore chunks of bone and flesh out of Layton's neck and chest!

I finally reacted by unloading a full clip of ammo into the monster with my K-9! The bullets breaking the Tiger's vice-like grip by slamming into his fifteen-inch head, causing him to let go! He pounced across the jungle floor like a house cat hit by a hive of stinging bees! He broke wide bolting back into the heavy undergrowth! On my way to what remained of Layton's body. I frantically went about reloading the K-9. At the same time, I tripped and fell into a large hole Charlie had dug out of the earth. It was cleverly, concealed with sticks and branches. I had fallen into a pit of punji sticks, sticks carved out of hard woods. Sharpen to a needle, point. With the tips of the sticks dipped with human feces to infect the wound. They were not in any order; they had placed them in all directions, to inflict as much damage to the human body as possible. I was lucky that the radio had fallen into the hole first and unlucky because one of the sticks had penetrated through the sole of my right boot. Driving the tip of the stick at least two inches into the ball of my foot and at a steep angle, I ended up with my ass sitting atop the radio, my K-9 landing just out of reach.

Suddenly, here came the Tiger again! However, it wasn't the same one. This one was smaller, possibly a female. I scrambled for my weapon, but couldn't reach it! She picked up what remained of Layton in her mouth and scrambled away with the remains! The ground is soaked with his blood; my heart is working overtime, pounding inside my chest as though it's trying to free itself from my rib cage! To complicate matters, I was hyperventilating; I had lost my breath during the excitement!

Finally getting my shit together, I managed to regain some measure of my senses. I stood upon my left foot being careful where I placed it! Using my right hand and leg muscles, I freed my right foot from the single stick and placed both feet evenly on the ground in the bottom of the hole! Using both hands, I climbed out of that goddamn pit wishing the sonofabitch who dug it were here so I could shoot his dumb ass! I reached down, picked up the radio, and laid it near the tree beside me. Then with a fresh clip in the K-9, I jammed a round into its chamber and began moving. Of course, I was scared shitless; my Pucker Factor had reached a new height of 90% with 10% being the highest on the scale. Yet, I realized I had to keep moving, going back to the edge of the ridge away from any other would be holes. I continued to move forward, ready to shoot anything that moved at this point. Watching the ground and my surroundings, I traveled only a few feet at a time along the ridge hoping my reaction time wouldn't fail me.

Then I heard the Tiger feeding to the left of me. I moved in staying glued to the tree trunks. No holes to worry about while standing on the roots of the trees around me, the male Tiger lay dying a few feet away from the female; she was down on all fours. The two of them had chewed Layton's body beyond all recognition. His head and upper torso was gone, what remained of him was, littered across the ground in front of me. His legs were being, eaten as if they were nothing more than large drum, sticks. His bones popping and snapping under the tremendous pressure of her powerful jaws, seeing me, she growled loudly, but kept feeding. I responded by going down on one knee, and taking careful aim. I unloaded on her head and down the side of her chest hoping I would hit something vital. She soared high into the air as the male had with the bullets stinging as they cut into her flesh! With lighting speed, I crammed another clip into the weapon as she turned and began charging me. I let loose this time aiming at her nose and eyes. Half way to me, she finally went down as the bullets dug into her skull and brain cavity.

In all of the commotion, I began jerking all over. My body was going into convulsions; I could not stop it, I was losing control of my senses! I just sat there for a few minutes trying to absorb everything that had happened, tears swelling.

I finally managed to get to my feet and slowly began making my way to Layton's remains, shoving my last clip into theK-9 as I went. There wasn't much left of him, his dog tags lay in a pool of blood under what remained of his rib cage. I bent over, picked up a lone dog tag and a ring lying next to it, and stuffed them into a pocket.

Only real things left to speak of were his boots. His feet still in them, one boot had his left leg sticking out of it. The leg had, been severed at the knee with the largest part of the flesh stripped to the bone. The other leg was, bitten off even with the top of his right boot.

I fell to my knees and started crying, I couldn't believe he was gone; I had no idea of what to say, or what to do.

My friend was gone. I just sat there staring with my hands on my knees looking at the bloody mess in front of me.

Reality slowly began coming back to me, I knew I had to get up and get out of there as quickly as possible. The male Tiger lay just a few feet away from me; he was groaning and gasping for air and slowly dying. That gave me one more thing to do before leaving. I walked to where the massive animal lay and stopped. Standing over him, I emptied the last clip into the side of his head screaming unintelligible words as his blood splattered everywhere, including on me!

I picked up Layton's boots and took them back with me to where I had left the radio. Once back at the tree, I put the radio across my shoulder, and then picked up Andy's K-9. Finding his ammo next to the hole, I had fallen into; I gathered it up slinging the belt over my free shoulder. Holding to Layton's boots, I untied the bootlaces, then tied the boots together and slung them over a shoulder with his K-9. Using a clip of his ammo, I reloaded my weapon. Placing the boot with his leg bone up to the knee behind me, when I walked the bone struck me in the back of the head. Adjusting the boot so that it hung lower down the back, I tried walking again. Done, I began making my way out of there again. My right foot is killing me with each step shooting pain all the way up my right leg. I was facing two enemies now, the Vietcong, and the wildlife. Being ate by the local beast or taken prisoner by the, Vietcong? Neither of those options was particularly appealing to me.

Finally coming to a drop in the soft earth, I made my way down the embankment to the sandy beach below.

Once there I heard something behind me! Driven totally by fear, I spun around on one foot and let go blasting the hell out of a large white bird.

"Shit!" I had just murdered an innocent bird; feathers flew in every direction. The feathers were still floating in the air when I keyed up the radio sending out a series of four clicks by the way of the talk button. Each hiss lasting about three-seconds each, and in less than a minute, I received two-hisses in return, indicating that an immediate extraction was on the way.

Like a Zombie. I just stood there waiting for my ride all the while watching those stupid white feathers floating in the air. It was as if they had a life of their own.

*We have superior weaponry! We have well-trained fighting
men! Weave tanks! We have vehicles! We have all types of
planes needed, and the means to deliver the bombs! What
we don't have is Politian's that will let us do our goddamn
jobs! Gen. LeMay was correct when
he said, 'We could bomb the Vietnamese
back into the Stone Age'. But he didn't count
on the weak, spineless and dim-witted
Politian's who are unable to find their
Assholes with both hands and a flashlight!
Idiots who insist upon making unwise and
Constant changes from behind safety
Of their Desk in Washington D.C...
Captain Carl W - Saigon*

CHAPTER ELEVEN

BACK AT BASE CAMP: WO (Warrant Officer) Johnson
sat the Huey down back at our camp cutting the engine.

I had Layton's boots in my lap. My camouflage
uniform covered with blood. The wind coming through
the open doors of the helicopter on the trip back had dried

it. The bright rich red color turned into a dark chocolate brown to almost black. I suppose I was in shock; I had made the ride back ok, but couldn't remember getting off the helicopter. I had the radio and Layton's boots on my back with both K-9s over one shoulder. Everything else I had apparently left behind.

Holding on to me, "SGT. Logan," Johnson said. "Let's go inside, have them look at you."

I heard the words, they just wasn't registering. Andy was all I could think of. What happened to him seemed surreal, like watching a movie, a fucked up movie, but a movie nonetheless.

The first face I saw was Peaches, once he learned that I had arrived back at camp, he came to meet me. I was standing half way between the helicopter and the entrance to the hospital with WO Johnson. He was still tugging at my arm trying to get me to walk.

Peaches approaching us, "God in heaven, what happened?"

Holding Layton's boots in my hands now, I finally started toward the M*A*S*H Unit. Peaches, was now at our side. He opened the door and as I walked in. Reyna, was the first to see me, she came in a dead run.

"Jack!" She said starting to cry, seeing all of the blood. Then nervously she began examining me with her eyes and her hands. "Are you okay?"

I was unable to respond.

Others gathered quickly, Maya was among them. Seeing the massive amount of blood, she began screaming believing that I was badly injured.

Dr. Major Phillips took Layton's boots from me. "We'll take care of these, son," handing them to a nurse, "Take care of these," then to Reyna. "Get him cleaned up and find him a bed, stat."

Reyna and Maya took the K-9s, the radio and pack placing them on a nearby Gurney.

Finally coming around a little, I helped to take my ammo belt off being careful with the grenades. Reyna and Maya were on either side of me as we headed for the showers at the end of the hall.

Once there they helped me to undress, Maya entered the shower stall with me. She's crying as she searches my body for any signs of being wounded.

Reyna left to get towels and a wheelchair. Blood began to gather on the floor as the scab on my foot began to soften. The bleeding began anew. Maya inspected it, cleaning the wound with soap and water. Then she began washing my hair.

I was getting sick, my nerves were finally settling down somewhat as the adrenalin began leaving my muscles returning them to normal. The pain was returning to my foot. The skin on and around it turned red and already began swelling. Infection was sitting in for a nice long visit.

Reyna returned with a hospital gown, towels, and the wheelchair. They made sure that I was dry before putting the gown on me. Then made me sit in the wheelchair, and placed a white towel under my foot. Reyna inserted a needle and started the IV.

Maya began taking my vitals. Then combed and tied my hair into a ponytail. At the same time, Reyna gave me a sedative that Dr. Phillips had ordered.

Then in a flash we were off to the operating room, once there they injected me with Demerol. Looking into Reyna's eyes my mind simply faded away.

Assigned to a bed on the ward, I slept for hours; I finally awoke because of the throbbing in my foot, with each throb of pain getting sharper.

I opened my eyes and saw Reyna sitting in a chair near my bed reading: Gordon Dickson's book, '*Soldier, Ask Not*', I stared at the cover of the book for a few minutes before turning my attention to her face. I watched her eyes as they darted left to right across the pages as she read, I stare at her long fingers with perfect polished nails turning each page once she had finished with them.

One way to get rid of the pain was too absorb it by thinking of something else entirely. I thought of Reyna's plush lips. "Hey you," I said softly.

She looked at me, got up putting the book aside, and then came to me. She sat on the bed laying her head across my chest at the same time.

With a hand to my face, "Are you alright?"

"Yeah, I think so."

"Savage and Higgins flew back with W.O. Johnson to where you were, attacked. They brought back the Tiger, the male I think they said. And the gear you left behind."

"Why?" I said. "The Tiger I mean."

"No idea, to make a comprehensive AAR report I suppose. Complete with pictures. But of course, I am never sure of what or why men do what they do."

"I could say the same about women."

Slowly, she moved her face to mine kissing me tenderly and changing the subject altogether. "When Lt. Higgins told us what happened to you, I was afraid. Then when I saw you in the condition you were in, I thought I may lose you." Her big blue eyes transfixed on me.

I did not answer, but I did notice she was wearing the necklace I had gotten her for Christmas.

"I have had you on my mind ever since you made that remark the other night."

"I have had you on my mind since the night we met at Hog's Hill," she said. "Do you remember that?"

"You're playing games again," I growled.

"It's true, and I am not playing any stupid game," she said firmly.

"Remember the remark you made back at the Christmas party?"

Questioning with, her eyes, "Remark?"

"You said that there was no Charles. What did you mean?"

She sat up on the edge of the bed taking my right hand into her left hand. "I also said that we needed to talk," with her mood darkening. "Charles died almost four years ago. I wear the ring and the name to ward off anyone who wants to get close to me." She said, brushing my uncombed hair from of my forehead with her long fingers. "After he died, I resigned myself to being alone."

"Dead…How…What happened?"

Shaking her head, "You know how he was always partying. I stopped partying after we got married. Because of that, we began growing apart since I thought he should grow up and told him so. We were not in high school anymore. To make things worse, he wanted a child. I had decided I wasn't going to do that, not with a drunk." She stood up straightening out her uniform. "I enrolled in nursing school at night, and during the day; I worked as a waitress at Louis's Coney." She glinted. "The police showed up one night telling me what had happened." Sitting next to me again, "Charles left the party with another girl to make a beer run. He lost control of the car and struck a tree killing them both."

"I'm sorry, I had no idea." I said. "But you can't hide yourself behind a ring and a name forever."

"I don't intend to," she said holding up her ring-less finger on her left hand. "Jack, can I ask you a personal question?"

I hadn't noticed she wasn't wearing the ring until that very moment, "Of course."

Hesitating, "How serious is your relationship with Maya?"

"I asked her to marry me, but I don't know."

"She said no?"

"Her mother said no to Maya. Her mother prearranged a marriage for her eleven years ago, according to Maya."

"Have you ever met her mother?" She continued.

"No, but I intend to."

"I would be interested in your assessment of her."

"Why's that?"

"Something is terribly wrong there. Maybe it's a woman's intuition, I don't know, but something is wrong." Her mood softening, "Do you remember that night in the hayloft? It was shortly after your grandparents had electricity installed in the old place."

"Are you kidding me? That was the first time that we made love. I will never forget that."

"I think of that night. Almost every day, it consumes me at times. How tender you were and how tender you are. A girl never forgets her first time," she laughed. "Do you remember that time Charles hit me and you kicked his ass? I pretended to be mad, but actually, it excited me. I have wished a thousand times. I would have come to you." She admitted. "And now look at us. I am an officer, and you are an enlisted man. It seems we can't get a break."

"I have so many thoughts running through my mind that I don't know exactly what to do or say. Maybe we were never, meant to be." Thinking back to Layton, "Destiny is a motherfucker."

"Do you think its destiny?" She asked.

"I don't know. What I do know is that I don't want to hurt Maya or you."

"I talked to Sergeant Savage and Major Baginski. I want to resign my commission and work for Sergeant Savage as a nurse. That way, we would have a chance to see where this would take us. Otherwise, I think I will lose my mind."

"I can't let you do that. You like the army as much as I do."

"I like the nursing, not necessarily the army. I love you and I want to be with you. I have given this a lot of thought Jack. And giving up my bars to be with you is a small sacrifice."

Well it worked, thinking about something else stop the pain sure enough. Now shock, replaced the pain. I didn't know what to say. All of a sudden, everything was clear.

"I am so sorry for being verbally mean to you. I apologize. I had no idea you felt this way."

"You do not owe me an apology. I had to work out my own issues and feelings," she said given me a long kiss. Pulling back, "You think about Maya, and whatever you decide, I will accept. My decision stands, as far as resigning my commission. I'd rather be in the wings waiting for you as a civilian, than a lieutenant knowing I would never have you."

"What if Maya and I work it out, then, what?"

She got to her feet, looked down at me avoiding the question, "I can wait for you, I've managed to wait this long."

* * * *

Although I was woozy when I awoke this morning, I still had Reyna's conversation from yesterday running through my mind like a freight train. To top it off, here was Maya insisting on giving me information she figured I needed to know.

"They take Commander Shore to Saigon, put into a care unit there. He never did speak while he was here, he speak there though." Wiping the sweat from my brow with a cool cloth, "The young girl you bring back is getting better, she say thank you."

"Good."

"The children have bounced back like rubber ball," smiling. "SGT. Savage is glad to have them here, he nice man," and on it went...

The woods are lovely, dark, and deep,
But I have promises to keep,
And miles to go before I sleep,
Robert Frost

CHAPTER TWELVE

MISSION: MA0835 WAR INCORPORATED: This Mission was a Search and Destroy mission, and no matter what happened or what was to come, it's officially filed as classified, meaning that no one could ever speak of it...

It has been a while since I have made any entries into the journal, mostly because nothing of any real consequence has happened over the past few weeks. A couple of routine missions and staying away from Reyna and Maya have pretty much taking up all of my free time. I did promise Maya when time permitted; I would go with her to talk to her mother about us getting married, although my interest in doing so was becoming less and less important to me.

Being honest with myself, I would prefer Reyna to spend the rest of my life with, not Maya. If only Reyna had been honest with me from the beginning, things may have turned out much differently. I couldn't put all of the blame on Reyna though. I was guilty of playing games myself, and it was eating me up inside with guilt over Maya. I cannot willfully hurt either of them. I believe that staying away from both of them may be the answer, at least until I can sort things out. I'm just not sure. I have tried not going into the field with this wrapped around my mind, because it could very well impede my performance. It hasn't yet, but I know it's coming, if I do not step up and get the matter settled.

* * * *

Back home, today it's 3 July 1966, the very first day TV News is to air at ten-o'clock in prime time; bringing the Vietnam War with even more gruesome details into the living rooms of the American late night viewers.

Here in Nam, it's already the next day, July Fourth. Exactly twenty-four hours ahead of the States, that means tomorrow, we can celebrate 4 July all over again. However, there is no celebrating today, for we are airborne and thirty-minutes away from our insertion point. If our Intel is correct, we should get in and out safely.

The rainy season had begun early; it would last well into September. I have a hate and love relationship with the rainy season, a paradox to be sure. At times, it rains for a month or more, sometimes three months solid. Light rain, medium rain, and at times it rained so hard you can't see your Johnson when you took a leak. Today the rain is light and intermittent.

As our Huey lowered itself into a steady hover over the jungle canopy below, the normal apprehension and fear of what may happen was settling in.

Higgins giving the signal, "It's time!" He Signaled.

Moments after checking our drop lines, four of us repelled down the secured ropes one after the other.

Hovering above the canopy with nowhere to land could at times be hazardous to one's health. This scared me more than any other part of the job. You had no way of knowing what waited for you on the jungle floor.

As each of us released the lines, we moved into the shadows of the jungle. Kneeling, searching, and observing the environment around us.

If Robert Frost had been a Ranger, he might have said:

'The Jungle is deadly, dark, and deep,
But I have a mission to keep,
And miles to go before I sleep'

We sat up a perimeter to protect the others coming down to join us. A light rain started a few minutes after everyone had cleared the lines, adding to the wet sogginess of the jungle floor. Within seconds of the last man letting go of the drop line, the pilot pulled straight up as the crew chief secured the ropes. Peaches turned and headed back to base. As repetitive as it had become, we waited until the chopper was out of earshot before starting our journey.

Lt. Higgins was SL (Squad Leader) again today. I haven't talked about him in detail. Nevertheless, he's thirty-six, he hails from Lubbock Texas. After a nasty divorce with his wife taking everything, he had. He returned to Vietnam as an advisor in late November 1963. Major Baginski recruited him in 1965 and has been with him ever since. Higgins is in for the long haul. A thirty-year-man, he had been in the shit on many occasions. Therefore, when he gave an order, we listened.

"Sarge," he said to me, his green eyes searching in the distance in front of us. "You and Baker take point;" he ordered. Looking up from his compass and indicating the direction with his right hand.

As ordered, Baker, Layton's replacement joined in on me. Together we began moving, staying in the shadows with Baker at point; I took the Slack Man's position staying twenty-five feet behind and to the left of him.

SGT. Brian Baker, a black-man fresh to the squad, is definitely one of the good guys. Before the Rangers, he was in college at Cal State prior to his stint in the Army. His mother died in an auto accident in 1963. Shortly after he joined the Army and went to school for communications, after two years of that he volunteered for the Rangers, and now here he is.

The jungle air is thick. The humidity sits at a hundred-percent. A white haze hangs in the air like an invisible curtain, making it hard to breath. With temperatures in the high nineties, everything we have on is wet. Our clothes clung to our bodies like, wet rags. Our thighs underarms and waists rubbed raw by the wet garments chaffing our skin.

Only minutes after the helicopter had left. The monkeys began their tree climbing, vine swinging and chattering in the overhead canopy.

Hearing the birds and animals was a good thing, it meant no one was in the immediate area, or at least no one we could see.

Major Baginski had found out first hand that dealing with the CIA was like dealing with the Mob. One favor deserved another. He knew that if a favor weren't reciprocated when asked for, someone would have to pay. On our last mission involving the Company, the Major had told them he would consider it a favor to let our team participate in another CIA classified mission.

The prior mission was, classified as top secret, which turned out a standard walk through occurrence. We assumed that the current mission would be the same. So like the Mob, The Company had asked for a favor from the Major.

Unfortunately, our team was at the bottom of the list as far as priority went, and probably never be, kept in the loop...a need to know type situation.

What we did know was that one of the Company's men; an Agent White had gone rouge according to the CIA. Our assignment was to find him, arrest him, and deliver him by force if necessary to a safe house near Saigon. Once there, agents would come and get him.

Agent White himself and Gen Hoi, a self-appointed leader of the Vietcong had worked out a drug and weapon exchange. White would furnish the weapons and Hoi would purchase them with drugs. Both men reported as being in a small Vietcong stronghold two-miles north of Nhân Trang in II Corp.

We were standing less than two-miles from our objective. Other than Agent White, there was a take no prisoner order. Intelligence had provided us with a recent photo of Hoi and White.

Intelligence reported Charlie's resistance to be very low in the village.

Making our way to the village, we received a radio transmission asking us to be on the lookout for a squad of fifteen Marines operating in the same area. They were, assigned to a nonrelated mission. As of this morning, the Marines were seventy-two hours overdue. If possible, they wanted us to make contact and have them report.

An hour later, we received another corrected report, stating that the morning report came in to command seven days ago, Government efficiency at its best...thereby, making the Marines eight-days overdue at this point.

Forty-five minutes passed, and we were closing to two-thousand-feet of where the village was located. We stopped. Hand-signals would continue to be our only form of communication from this point forward; voices would carry for great distances.

Smells are very important in the jungle, no smoking, hair tonic, toothpaste, deodorant. No soap, foot powder, shaving cream, chewing products, nothing, just your unwashed skin is allowed in the jungle, as per Baginski's orders.

Forty more minutes passed before we stopped. The odor of death filtered through the air. One thing about death, human or animal, the odor is similar. Giving the signal, we dispersed putting twenty-foot intervals among all squad members. SGT Baker and I still shared the point. Slowly, we inched our way to the mouth of a small clearing and stopped again.

Our eyes quietly searching in the distance, it was then we saw them. Bloated bodies of soldiers tied to trees. Baker and I closed in, yet stayed concealed in the jungle foliage. The others remained hidden in the surrounding plant life in a large semi-circle.

Regrettably, we had located the band of overdue Marines. Their clothes cut from their bodies; some had their pants down to their ankles. One in particular had U.S.M.C. tattooed across the top of his right shoulder. The dead numbered exactly fifteen. They had been decapitated, and disemboweled. Their entrails lay on the ground in front of them bearing signs of being, ravaged by the wildlife. Their heads sat into their empty C cavities, their penis, and testicles cut away and stuffed into their mouths. The bodies were, discolored and blackened.

Thank God, this scene would never make it into the living rooms back home, at least I hoped not. We didn't see any explosives near the bodies, even though the Vietcong liked to booby trap everything. However, in this case the animals tearing at the dead would have set off any explosives. I saw a medic pouch laying to the left of the last body, a US Navy Man no doubt, since the Marines didn't have medics of their own. The Marines are shoeless, no dog tags nor weapons were seen.

The Vietnamese believed if they dismembered their enemy's body, their enemies could not be reborn to come back to fight them in another life. Believing their spirits is doomed to roam the outer realm forever. Knowing this didn't keep back the tears of anger from swelling within us. We wanted payback.

Without prior notice, a low muffled noise came from thirty-feet northeast of our position. Like turning off a TV set, the animals went quiet; the only sound left was a flock of birds taking flight through the treetops. We stepped back into the shadows; silently we began encircling the area in the direction the sound had come from. Shafts of light filtered through the leafy green canopy overhead, striking the ground and the brown and reddish green trees around us. Grapevines hung from the branches overhead. They were alive with a variety of snakes curling and twisting as they made their way up the branches searching for food.

Baker was on the left, I was on the right as we moved forward. Silently, and carefully placing our feet as we went. We stopped without giving any signals. The smell had changed from death to the faint aroma of Limburger Cheese, or Arm Pit Juice, (Tiger Balm). Homemade by the Vietnamese and worn to ward off evil spirits.

The smell signifying that Charlie was close by, Baker held up his left hand, pointing back south, in the direction we had come from.

We observed two Vietcong draped in black wearing their traditional straw „Non la's, (Conical Hats). Both men were on their knees behind a fallen tree hiding from us. A .30 caliber machine-gun affixed to a metal tripod sat in front of them, just behind the log. They had set up an ambush to kill anyone approaching the bodies. A basic ambush tactic the Vietcong often used. Soldiers would come along and find their friends in a position like the Marines. Seeing their plight, they would frequently go ballistic for what had befallen their comrades; Charlie would take advantage of the situation by unleashing a barrage of gunfire and grenades.

Lt. Higgins waiting in the wings, made a deliberate noise drawing the Vietcong's attention in his direction. Baker and I slowly closed the gap between them and us. They had no idea we were there. We walked right up to them. We stood there watching them like coiled snakes ready to strike.

My guy resisted by pounding his head against the butt of my K-9 until he lost consciousness.

Baker took a more simple approach; he just choked his partner out. Done, we sat motionless for a few seconds listening for any other activity that may be taking place in the immediate area. It took two minutes or so for the monkeys to start climbing trees, chattering and vine swinging.

The two men armed with the Czech's version of the AK-47, had two Marine issue K-Bar knives lying beside them on the ground. They were guilty of the death of the Marines by association if nothing else.

We dragged the two unconscious men back to the clearing, and away from the dead soldiers. I tossed both K-bars at Higgins feet before trying to wipe the cheese smell off my hands.

Higgins looked at the knives; then taking water from his canteen, he splashed it in their faces. One awoke immediately, and began choking and spitting, while the other coiled into a fetal position and began moaning in pain.

"Đung nói cho bat cu đieu gì nguoi My!" (Do not tell the Americans anything!") He said to his friend still lying on the ground.

"Làm the nào đen nay là làng cua ban?" (How far is your village?) Higgins asked.

Neither of the prisoners acknowledged the question.

"How far is your village?" Higgins repeated in English.

There was no response.

Higgins motioned to Baker. Baker knelt down on one knee beside the man I had disarmed. He grabbed him by the hair of his head, pulling him up into a sitting position. The little man held onto Baker's arm with both hands. Before the man realized what was about to happen, Baker ripped his left ear from his head, covering the little man's mouth with an open palm to quiet his screams.

The blood oozed from the gaping wound, the lesion ran half down the side of his face. He was squirming, trying his best to get free.

"Đoi! Đung giet chúng tôi cho ban biet nhung gì ban muon biet." (Wait! Don't kill us I tell you what you want to know). "There!" He pointed toward the ridge behind us suddenly speaking English. "Only old people and children are in village," his eyes widened at the prospect of what Baker might do to him.

"Where is Gen Hoi?" Higgins continued.

The prisoner wiping tears, replied, "He not there," he gulped. "Left two days ago for Cam Ranh Bay, he is there."

"Where in Cam Ranh?"

"He with CIA general man White."

"Sonofabitch! Sonofabitch!" Higgins cursed quietly, and then turned back to the prisoner. "Gen Hoi has opium, heroin, and smoking weed?"

"Yes," the small man, confirmed.

Higgins pointing to the Marines, "Did Hoi do this?"

"No."

"Who did?"

"Vietcong here last week, took all young men and girls from village. They killed the Marines."

"And where were you and your buddy?"

"With Gen Hoi, not in Village, but in Nha Trang, Gen Hoi upset when he returns."

We knew that they were lying in order to save their lives. Both men were set to ambush us and both were probably guilty of killing the Marines, or at least participated. Looking at the dead Marines, we turned our attention back to the two gooks. Using our knives, we quietly killed them.

Into the radio, "Raven One - this is Angel Six, come-in - Over." Higgins clearly upset.

Static, then suddenly, "Angel Six, this is Raven, go-ahead - Over."

Higgins gave the coordinates as to where to locate the missing detail of Marines. Information given, Higgins asked that Major Baginski meet us at Cam Ranh Bay. With a request for an extraction to stand by, once we were at the extraction point, we would call again.

Higgins sent SGT. Jonathan Jack and Joseph to do a reconnaissance mission around the village, instructing them to meet us at the extraction point.

* * * *

Once in the air, Higgins was on the radio talking to the Major. By the time, we made it to the extraction point, giving our exact position; and popping green smoke at the LZ. Almost an hour had passed. SGT. Jack and Joseph had returned without incident only to report the status of the camp. It was as the two dead men had said. No one was in the village of any consequence.

Therefore, this day, the village would not be bombed, but left intact.

Another hour passed before the pilot sat us down on a landing pad at Cam Ranh near the 402st Security Agency Special Operations Detachment Airborne Unit; next door to the Temporary office for Military Intelligence and field Office for the CIA.

Gear in hand; we climbed down from the Huey as the power to the engine was, cut. The blades began to wind down as we spotted Major Baginski who was there to greet us.

"Lieutenant!" Baginski said smiling. "Everyone, make it back ok?"

"Yes sir, all safe and sound. The village only had a few old people and kids in it, appears Hoi is using the village as his home base."

Still smiling, Baginski turned his attention to us. "Gentlemen, hanger 16 has been set up for you. Showers and newspapers from back home, the whole nine yards. Get settled in. Later we'll have a sit down," he concluded.

"Yessir," we answered together.

The four of us trekked off in the direction of the hanger where a small fixed wing L19 sat just outside of the hanger doors. A short but stubby aircraft mechanic was removing the plane's engine cowling. Memories of being an aircraft mechanic flashed through my mind. *Could be me doing that boring ass job*, I was thinking.

The Major and Higgins headed to the small office complex near the radio tower.

"What's going on guys?" Joseph asked as we walked.

"The Situation Normal, bud, All Fucked Up. (SNAFU) I said.

"The lieutenant seemed upset," Joseph, continued. "I took his reaction as we would have to hunt for those two? I take it he wanted this to be quick and easy."

"What's wrong with quick and easy," shifting my pack to my other shoulder? "Isn't that the way you like your women?"

"Fuck you."

"Who gives a shit? Let's just get a shower, eat, and dry the fuck out." SGT. Jack complained, coming up from behind. "Besides, I need some Vaseline for my balls!"

Baker laughed. "Man, you're on your own there, bud."

The food was good, roasted chicken with rice, mashed potatoes and gravy, hot rolls, meatloaf with three choices of vegetables and desert, coffee, tea, milk, and ice water filling out the menu, not bad, not bad at all.

Entering the hanger, we staked out two of the twelve tables and piled our gear on them; we found an assortment of fresh civilian clothing, underwear, trousers, and shirts on another table for us until our laundry was, done.

As the Major had said, there was a stack of newspapers on the floor beside the clothes. The papers were from New York, Chicago, and California. News articles and photos covered the front pages of Negros killed and churches burned out shells. The Ku Klux Clan in Alabama said to be at fault. Baker was busy studying one newspaper in particular.

Later, Lt. Higgins and Major Baginski entered the hanger through the back door stopping at the buffet table. They too filled their plates. I returned for strawberry pie to go with my fifth glass of chocolate milk. They had their heads together, whispering and glancing at the rest of us as they made their way to an empty table. We went about the business of finishing our meals and policing the area. (Picking up trash)

The enlisted man's laundry room was available to us; even though our clothes were wet from humidity, at least they were clean. A shower and a shave made us feel almost human again after three weeks in the bush.

More than thirty-minutes passed before the Major was ready to speak, getting to his feet, he walked to the front. "All right men," he said with Higgins following. "Take a seat over here. I want everyone up front."

Without a word, we did as asked leaving our gear where it lay. Baker brought the newspaper with him.

"Gen Hoi is here with Agent White. As you were, briefed, Gen Hoi has a cache of drugs that Agent White is going to purchase from him. He, is planning to transport the drugs back to the US for sale on the streets of America, Baginski sighed. "It's a good thing that we have a, to kill order for Gen Hoi. At least we can prevent him from doing this type of a thing again. If the shit gets thick out there, just remember that we still have an arrest assignment for White." The major's mood was somber. "The lieutenant and I went out on a limb. We lied our asses off telling Agent White that we had been searching for him in order to offer him a deal. We told him that we would be happy to provide him and Gen Hoi with security and transportation for a fee. Offering them a helicopter ride to Saigon, or anywhere else, convincing White that no one would ever know. We told him we would be happy to help him in any of their future business ventures as well. They bought it hook line and sinker," he said. Continuing the Major added. "We came up with a plan of our own, once we have both White and Hoi at Hoi's encampment, and as soon as Hoi makes his cache of drugs available to White. We will complete our mission and destroy Hoi and the drugs.

After a long pause, the Major took a long drink of water. "There could be some serious repercussions if we screw this up. I am fully prepared to face any consequence, which may come. I will do this alone if necessary, but I could use some help." He continued. "If any man here chooses to step aside, I'll understand. You will be reassigned to another duty post, no questions asked."

We looked at each other for a few seconds before I raised my hand.

"Yes, Logan," the Major responded.

"When do we leave, Sir?"

Pausing the Major waited for any other comments before adding, "0500."

Joseph got to his feet. "Sir, is it possible to get another meal out of these dickheads before leaving in the morning?"

Baginski smiled. "Chow is at 0400 Sergeant."

"Thank you, Sir."

* * * *

0400 ZULU - It's July 4 Back Home. Some of us were already up and watching as the people on KP duty are carrying the chow in. They sat everything up on a table at the far end. Shit on a Shingle, (SOS) scrambled eggs, grits, gravy, bacon, and biscuits.

I'm thinking about people back home enjoying their weekend off. Some heading north, going fishing, or just visiting family. On the farm, Joseph and I never had a vacation we were always working.

Baker sat down beside me, breaking my train of thought by giving me a carton of milk. He laid his newspaper down in front of me. "Check this shit out," he said with a grim look. "The motherfuckers killed nine men and women, three girls, eight, eleven, and thirteen, and burnt their church to the ground! My family? I don't know if they are ok or not."

"You know the Major would be the first to get you through to the States. We can go to him, and he'll let you call." I explained.

"What the fuck am I doing here, Jack? Those assholes are killing my people while my black ass and others like me are over here fighting for our country! It's not right!" Slamming his fist down on the table, "It's bullshit, man!"

"We will get the major, make the phone call."

SGT. Jonathan Jack joined us overhearing, Bakers remarks. He sat quietly drinking a cup of coffee listening to Baker's complaints.

Jonathan Jack was a full-blooded Navaho Indian originally from Nevada; his father had been a high steel worker in New York. Once Jack graduated high school, his father was, transferred to Vegas to help build a new skyscraper casino, giving him a large raise in pay and benefits to do so. SGT. Jack left there and joined the Army; he had no interest in that line of work.

He interjected the trials and tribulations of the Indians in the American West to Baker trying to make him feel better. I left to prepare for the helicopter trip leaving them behind to solve the world's racial problems.

By 0930, we had two-Hueys' in the air. An hour into the flight, we were closing in on a landing zone six miles northeast of Saigon. The Major and, Lt. Higgins, White and Gen Hoi were in the lead helicopter. This would be the first time most of us would be in the same proximity of the Vietcong as friendly's, we were not at all comfortable with the situation.

It finally dawned on my dumb ass as to why the shower's and laundry. The Major wanted us to appear as soldiers fresh out of the rear and not combat veterans. I just hoped we had the, where with all needed to pull it off. Gen Hoi's men would be there, approximately twenty or so strong according to, Hoi. They were his men and we would be totally at their mercy if anything went wrong.

Agent White assured the Major that Hoi would hold up his end. Seems Hoi held more value in money than he did in killing his enemy.

We were flying about five-feet above the treetops heading southeast when the lead Huey-made a long right-turn.

I watched Baker sitting across from me as he went about honing the edge on his knife with a fine oiled stone. He had made his call. He was able to speak with his Dad in Alabama, which pleased Baker for the moment. As anyone could see, the matter was far from being resolved.

The pilot pulled back on the cyclic stick and turned down the RPM'S on the collective, we slowed from ninety-knots to forty-knots in a matter of seconds. We could see a group of hooch's in the distance with rice-paddies extending out beyond the buildings. As soon as we were on the ground and unloaded, the pair of Huey's was up, and away.

Gen Hoi climbed out of the lead chopper wearing a wide smile, everyone else including White followed. Hoi's uniform fit his small frame well. If you didn't know the man was an asshole, you would think of him as a professional soldier.

Baginski, Higgins, and Hoi were talking as if they were lifetime friends. After a few minutes, Baginski excused himself, and moved over to where we were awaiting orders.

"Heads up men," Baginski said in a low voice. "I radioed ahead. The Foo-gas will be on two 2 ½ ton trucks and will be here soon." (Foo- Gas a mixture of explosives JP-4 and napalm, usually two fifty-gallon drums as one set.) Wiping the sweat from his face with a shirtsleeve, "Two of the Marine's finest will be driving the trucks. They have been, briefed, and hopefully will be ready to respond on our signal. Hoi's expecting five trucks. We want him to believe the two trucks are the first of the five."

"Yessir," we agreed.

Finally, Hoi gave an order for his men to show themselves and they did. Twenty-two, being the final count appearing one and two at a time from the surrounding buildings and tree lines, all we could do at present was to assume this was all of them until we were at the ready.

These assholes were combat hardened vets. Their faces bore witness to it. I'm sure they will be able to see it in some of us. As an act of intimidation, they wore the dog tags of our fallen soldiers around their necks in plain view. As hard as it was at that moment, we had no choice but to ignore it.

We smiled, giving them space as we milled around like cows awaiting slaughter, while waiting for Hoi's orders.

A short time later, Hoi finally pointed, ordering his men to remove the lumber coverings beneath several of the huts.

Being on higher ground, the rainwater flowed away from the huts, leaving the ground beneath dry. Dirt with plants covered each piece of the stacks of lumber in such a way it looked like normal ground beneath them. The plants and the dirt placed in random patterns was a very clever camouflage indeed. There were several such huts, used in this manner, each one hiding its own cache of drugs and weapons.

Hoi wanted the cargo concealed from eyes above, so once the drugs were, removed from their hiding places. He ordered us to move everything seventy-five-yards away to the first hill at the top of the beginning rice paddy. By placing them under the over-hanging trees and foliage, his goal would be complete. We joined in with helping hands, this chore taking a little over an hour to complete.

Almost at the same moment, the two trucks arrived from Saigon. Major Baginski stopped them in front of the huts until the loading was to commence. We could not let Hoi or his men see the explosives in the back of the trucks for obvious reasons.

After a few minutes, Hoi shouted to the Major and Agent White that he was ready for the first truck.

The drugs would be loaded first and then the weapons on the rest of the trucks that would never come.

We did our part to continue with the farce, we carried our weapons at ease. Then scattered out moving toward the lead truck as it turned around and began backing up. We busily started shouting out directions, and guiding, the truck backwards with hand signals, all the while, maneuvering ourselves into an attack position.

The canvass on the back of the truck flapped loosely in the wind, we hoped the enemy would believe the truck was empty. The Marine from the second truck had nonchalantly moved into position with the rest of us careful to stay away from any friendly fire positions, but moved as he was going to help with the loading. Some of us had learned their M-16's against a tree or a crate while moving the drugs, but keeping them well within reach. I carried the K-9 across my shoulder.

Suddenly, one of Hoi's men moved to the rear of the truck dropping its tailgate while the truck was still in motion. His expression went blank once he saw the explosives. He responded instantly with his AK47 coming up to fire, in the same moment. We rolled our weapons up and cut loose while still others made mad dashes grabbing their weapons.

As the gunfire erupted on both sides, we had to pick out our targets in a split second while they were running and moving, firing without hesitation or reservation.

Major Baginski had taken Agent White by surprise, knocking him to the ground with the butt of his pistol to the head. Baginski locked White's right hand, to the metal step of a jeep with handcuffs. Searching White's body, he found a .32 Cal pistol, tossing it aside. With White secure, Baginski took out both forty-fives, and joined the battle. With both handguns pumping he took out three of the Vietcong as he ran toward them, at the end of this day, he would be better known as, Johnny Fuckin' Wayne!

The second Marine had brought the truck to an abrupt stop, bailed out hitting the ground rolling into a prone position; he took out four of them before we realized that he was even there.

The intense firefight perused with some of our people being, hit, there was no time to access whom.

Dust flew as rounds dug into the ground around us. Tree bark splitting and shattering as the projectiles ripped into them while others whizzed by overhead. After taking down two others, Baker and I focused on this one guy; he came rushing our position with his AK barking! Why he hadn't hit us, I will never know. We hit this asshole with every bullet, but he refused to go down! The rounds were tearing through his body with blood and meat splattering! I couldn't believe that neither of us had hit a vital organ, he was still coming! An aura of red spray silhouetted his body! Baker's, final shot struck the man in the head just above his right eye. Stopping him cold, he fell face down in the mud and slid toward us.

Simultaneously, we reloaded as quickly as possible; and never stopped firing until the last one of Hoi's men was down. Our hearts were pumping like sledgehammers in our chest. Those of us still standing, shot rounds into the heads of each of the fallen VC, insuring all were as they should be, dead. We had taken Agent White, Gen Hoi and his men by surprise. We were not lucky, we were, blessed this day; the whole thing could have turned out so much differently than it had, and we knew it. Hoi lay dead at the bottom of the pile.

SGT. Jack had taken two rounds to his left leg, with another through the center of his right foot. Pieces of what was left of his foot hung from the stump of his ankle.

Joseph had taken a round through the top of his boot, but the injury didn't appear to be serious.

Higgins tended to their wounds while the rest of us went about unloading the explosives.

No time to call for a Medevac, we had to move. We were very aware that the firefight would bring more Vietcong regulars to the area to investigate the goings on. We still needed time to destroy the drugs before we left the area. Both drivers helped with the unloading and placement of our small arsenal.

Baker and I helped the two Marines and Lt. Higgins place the two fifty-five-gallon drums of JP4 and, Napalm at either edge of the medium size paddy. Baginski and the others made sure all of the drugs were inside the paddy. Once they were, Baker and I placed six claymores with the exploding side facing the drums. Then we went about the task of placing a number of trip wires in as many directions as possible in an attempt to achieve the maximum kill effect. Once all of the drugs were in place, we poured three fifty-five-gallon drums filled with JP-4 into the water of the rice paddies at the top of the hill. The genius and almost perfect engineering of the rice paddies provided the maximum flow of the fuel down one paddy and then the other until it flowed down to the bottom of the hillside. Once one of the claymores was, tripped, the explosion would trigger a chain of events. The claymores would set off the Napalm and the JP-4 causing the fire and Napalm to explode into a-flaming-hell.

Napalm burns until it burns itself out, there is no extinguishing Napalm, which meant the drugs would be nothing more than chemical waste when done.

Hurriedly, we climbed into the trucks and headed for Saigon at a rapid clip. Twenty-two minutes into the trip, someone had found our claymores. We saw a large hellish red ball of fire; boil into the sky.

CHAPTER THIRTEEN

SAFE HOUSE: We made to Saigon without incident. We received good news from the doctors at the Saigon Hospital for Joseph; the wounds to his left leg were superficial, as we all had hoped. They bandaged him up and gave him a tetanus shot and some pain pills. Then released back to the squad, SGT. Jack however, was not so lucky, they took him into surgery right away, and an hour later, a doctor came out telling us the bullets had shattered the bones in his ankle. Expressing the fact that they had to remove the rest of his foot just above the ankle, we never got to say goodbye to him. Due to complications, they took him back to surgery while they were in the process of releasing Joseph.

The doctor told us the army would return SGT. Jack to the states and medically discharge him with a pension. We hoped he would at least write and let us know what was going on with him from time to time.

In short, order, they shuffled us off to the rear for some R&R at a small camp south of Saigon while we waited. Baginski was to contact the CIA when he was prepared to have White picked up. He wanted us to rest up and be fresh in case something went wrong. Higgins said that three days should do the trick. The camp had served as a part time resting place for the Special Forces (Sneaky Pete's) who had been operating in the area.

We found a broken meat locker inside the unused mess hall in the east of the compound, which would serve as a jail cell for White. Was nothing more than a steel room with no windows, and only one door that locked from the outside, the smell was rancid, but we knew White would not mind. Mainly, because we didn't give a shit if he liked it or not. Lt. Higgins took it upon himself to watch over White when he needed to use the latrine or eat. Secretly hoping White would make a break for it so he could dispose of the bastard.

The small post was well equipped the barracks had TV, radios and fresh food in the fridge. A rack filled with magazines from back home, all of the amenities we could ask for. The conditions were very comfortable to say the least. We spent the night doing what we wanted, showers being the first on the agenda. We ate and lay around as if we were living the Life of Riley for the rest of the night.

SGT. Baker watched the news stations trying to try to find out what was happening back in Alabama.

We were up at 0530 brushing our teeth all the while enjoying the new uniforms and boots brought over by the 354th Transportation Unit out of Saigon at 0800. I was especially pleased they had brought in more sox. I was also pleasantly surprised to find chocolate milk stuffed into the fridge, my personal favorite of the milk line.

Our mail had, been forwarded to us. Handing, Baker a letter from home, it struck me as being odd, but it had no meaning at that particular moment. I thought it strange the Major didn't want anyone knowing that we were here yet.

0930, we reported to the mess hall for a meeting with Major Baginski and Lt. Higgins as requested. The two Marines who had helped us in Hoi's camp were in the front row. Baker brought his letter along with him to the meeting.

"Men," Baginski began. "How many of you got mail within the last hour?" A show of hands went up. "I apologize but I believe I have involved you in something we may not get out of so easily. White's people know that we have him, as well as our location." Clearing his throat, he pointed to the two Marines who had driven the trucks, "Sergeant's Slavin and Smith will remain with us until we are done here, once done, we will drop them off at their base camp."

Their home base is at the Forward Operating Base 1 - located just south of Phu Bai in I Corps. SGT. Slavin is from Florida, he and his teammate bunked with Joseph, Baker, and me last night. Baker and Slavin had spent most of the night talking about being back in the world so they could do their thing.

SGT. Smith was the moody type he didn't do much talking. The reason for that according to Slavin was, Smith had helped with the torching of a village a few months back, said that he had not been the same since.

"So now what," Higgins purposed.

"We will be ready for them when they get here," Baginski said. "We know what needs to be done, so let us get to it. The Marines can help."

"Yes sir," Higgins pointing to the Marines, "Come with me people."

As usual, it's pouring rain, once outside, Baginski, Joseph and I went about setting up the claymores we had taken from the supply shack. We sat six in a circle at the helicopter pad attaching a Clacker (Trigger Device) to the system. Then we sat out more claymores in the event any wheel vehicles might accompany the chopper in a quest to free, White. Attaching an additional Clacker to those, we didn't know how or even for sure if someone would come, but we planned for the worst-case scenario as a precaution. Our training had taught us to have a backup plan to our back up plan. Therefore, we planned another backup plan to that backup plan we had and planned for that plan. Damn, I wouldn't want to say all of that again.

Lt. Higgins placed the two Marines in firing positions fifty-meters apart giving them a field of fire, east, and west. They overlooked the helicopter landing pad and the front entrance of the mess hall.

The rest of us were to take up positions, covering every angel of approach from that point. Knowing exactly what the enemy as we had classified them, may be planning to hit.

Once positioned in the bush, we crouched down in the pouring rain with our ponchos on and waited.

1100 and so far a no show, which didn't mean much, the heavy rain was a considering factor; reducing the visibility considerably, especially if they were coming in by chopper.

Baginski was busy making the rounds checking to assure everyone is in their proper place, he settled in next to Joseph and waited with us.

Fifteen-minutes later, we heard the faint noise of a Huey approaching from the north.

Obscured by the rain and fog we still couldn't see it.

Baginski exited the bush moving toward the landing pad. If it were our guest coming, he had intended on greeting them as if nothing was wrong. If they indeed had release forms for him to sign, he would gladly give White over to them. That way we could be on our way back home, he didn't want an incident, but he was prepared if one materialized.

The Huey came in at a hundred-feet hovering like a giant locust, the pilot made his decent as if he was at the controls for the first time. As if he was attempting his first landing, what he was actually doing was killing time.

Joseph threw a rock at me to get my attention; two jeeps were coming in from the east. Two men in each of them, and using the noise from the chopper to cover the sounds of their approach.

The chopper continued it's decent as the jeeps closed the distance between them and us.

Baginski is no man's fool; he gave the signal by waving a friendly gesture at the chopper as he backed away from the well-placed claymores to the safe zone. He's standing just inches away from the trigger mechanism. He had learned well from the ambush tactics of the Vietcong.

The chopper landed cutting its engine, with the spin of the rotor blades slowing; creating a small tropical storm of their own. Five armed men in uniform jumped from the Huey with weapons aimed at Baginski.

"Get on your knees, Major! Now!" The lead man ordered.

Baginski obeyed the order instantly, going down on his knees, his right knee hitting the Clacker. "Blooommm!" The bad guys and the Huey exploded into a blazing inferno!

Baginski rolled into a large watery mud hole away from the leaping flames!

The men in the jeeps had jumped out and closing on the major blasting away; together we took three of them out.

The driver in the second jeep hit the gas putting the jeep into a tailspin as he tried getting away. The two Marines stood up and shot at the lone driver with automatic M-16 rifle fire. With the driver dead, the vehicle ran into a ditch and overturned.

Mud covered and rain soaked, Baginski waited until we made sure the area had, been cleared before he moved away from his spot.

"Lieutenant!" Baginski grimaced wiping his face smearing the mud. "Bring that sonofabitch out here immediately, please!"

"Yes Sir," Higgins began his journey toward the meat locker. With only minutes passing, he returned from the meat locker with White in hand.

Higgins removing his handcuffs, "I see that you have come to your senses, Major. Those were only the first to come for me. I admit, they were not of your caliber, but there will be others. You can't kill them all!"

"I don't intend to," Baginski said removing one of his forty-fives. Then in the blink of an eye, shot White in the forehead, his head exploded as his lifeless body bolted backwards into the mud landing on his back.

Putting away the pistol, his eyes fixed on White when he said. "Lieutenant, call command and tell those assholes that it is with great regret, that Agent White has been killed in a foiled escape attempt. Give them a body count and then call Peaches. Tell him to get us the fuck out of here."

"Yes Sir."

* * * *

On the way, we dropped the two Marines off at their base as promised. I will miss those guys. They had followed orders without question. They had taken what had happened in stride. When Lt. Higgins asked them to keep what had happened back there to, themselves. SGT. Slavin replied, "Simper Fi, Motherfucker! Marines don't squeal."

I thought that his remarks were right on target, but Higgins just sighed.

Five-hours later and after a bone bouncing helicopter ride, we were finally home. SGT. Baker and I went to the barracks where we settled in for a short rest.

Later, while on the way to the mess hall, we stopped at the command center in order to check the mission board. We discovered that we were up again first thing tomorrow morning.

"When are we ever going to catch a break?" Baker complained.

"When hell freezes over," Joseph catching up with us.

Since we had to be in the Mission Briefing room at 0600, we spent the rest of the evening restocking our rucksacks and making ready for tomorrow's mission. It was after ten before the rain finally slacked up leaving the night air thick and hard to breathe.

Although we sat around in our boxer shorts playing cards, it was still hot and sticky.

"Rummy," Baker smiled laying out his hand on the table.

"Damn man, you sure you're not cheating?" Joseph accused tossing his cards across the table.

I laughed but Baker didn't think too much of his comment. "Man, what do you hillbilly grit eating motherfuckers know about playing cards anyway?"

"Apparently not to fuckin much," Joseph shot back.

Baker and I laughed.

At the same moment the door at the main entrance opened, and in stepped a replacement for SGT. Jack. His gear in hand, he was soaked to the bone.

"Hi guys, SGT. Glass from the 101st," he said removing his rucksack.

"Welcome to the squad, Glass," Baker responded. "Pick a bunk."

"Anywhere?"

"Anywhere," I offered.

"Thanks guys."

Right behind him, the door opened again. It was Maya standing on the first step, "Chao."

(Hi) she said to me.

I excused myself joining her outside, after I had put on my pants; we walked to a place where we couldn't be overheard.

"Ban khoe không?" (How are you?) She asked.

"I see you have forgotten how to speak, English?"

She bowed her head. "Sorry."

"No need to be sorry, its ok."

"I have miss you."

I smiled. "I have miss you too."

She laughed. "Sorry again, I mean missed," she corrected.

"So why are you here?"

"I here because I love you, I here because no matter what mother say. I want to marry you."

"It's okay, I understand tradition, I don't like it, but I understand it," trying again to avoid what I had gotten myself into.

"Not good for me! I love you, not Dimn; I have never met him, so how could I love him?"

"And that leaves us where?"

"Leave us?"

"What do we do now?"

She grabbed me hugging me with both of her arms around my waist. "I love you, I want only you."

I kissed her on top of her head, thinking to myself. What was I going to do? I want Reyna, God what a mess I had made of things.

"When get back, you go with me, talk to mother?"

"Yes," agreeing reluctantly, trying not to sound disinterested.

"Nhung gì?" (What?)

"Yes. I will go with you and talk to your mother."

We spent a little more time together before I told her I had to go; I could see the hurt and doubt in her eyes. She could tell that I was blowing her off. Then I realized I couldn't do it, she hadn't done anything to deserve this. To mask my true feelings we made out for a while before we finally said goodnight.

Speak or act with an impure mind
And trouble will follow you.
Buddha

CHAPTER FOURTEEN

MA9043 RECON Vietcong STRONGHOLD: Near Pleiku:

As morning came, we only had time for a quick shower, leaving our socks and underwear behind this time. We headed for the highlands where the Montagnard, the people of the Highlands lives. Or the Nùng, (A tribes people of Chinese origin from the highlands of North Vietnam, some of whom moved south).

The fabric of our uniforms soaked up the water; it so happens that in the mountain regions not wearing any under garments prevented certain kinds of funguses. Since they had pushed up the mission, we left before I had time to talk to Maya. I had received word that she was waiting for me at the mess hall. Nevertheless, the way it worked out; I was unable to meet her. I hoped

SGT. Savage would explain to her that they had sent us out early.

Pleiku is, hidden deep in the Central Highlands, of the Truing Son Mountains. The mountain's elevations vary from eight-hundred feet and smaller. The NVA and the Vietcong believed whoever controlled the mountain ranges controlled South Vietnam. The Vietcong had many successful ambushes against our troops along Highway 19. The Ho Chí Minh Trail was a vital link between Pleiku and Qui Nhon. They had defended this road going all the way back to the French, never suffering a closing. Our troops were, sent there continuously to strengthen our hold on Highway 19, a case of history repeating itself.

In 1965, there was a military base at Pleiku housing a few hundred military and indigenous personnel. The Vietcong overran the base killing and taking what prisoners they wanted along the way. This attack had helped push the United States involvement in to the Vietnam Conflict.

The highlands were thick and green. Constant rains during the rainy season kept it that way. The areas of course are abundant with wildlife, especially the elephant. SGT. Layton and the episode with the Tiger came to mind. Every time I had entered a less-traveled path in any jungle area. I had to think of it as lightening not striking twice in the same place, hoping it would never happen again.

The 4th Infantry Division operated in the same area, but our orders stated that we were not to make contact with them. We were to evade any contact with the NVA, the Vietcong as well. We were simply to get in, Recon, find out what Charlie was up to, and get the hell out. We had seven days to cover a twelve-mile area north of Pleiku and report what we found, A-sap.

Plasmodium falciparum is a form of malaria in the highlands; all of us had taken our Dapsone (diamino-diphenyl sulfone) before leaving our main base. Dapsone actually is a leprosy medicine, yet it worked well in preventing malaria. We had ample supplies with us for daily doses. This didn't cover the big orange pill, better known as the Monday Morning Pill. It had Quinine in it, which had a tendency to turn the skin a yellowish color. The same ingredients found in Tonic Water for mixing alcohol drinks. Some doctors prescribe small amounts of Tonic Water for leg cramps in the elderly.

On a sad note, Tate just received a radio transmission that SGT. Glass, Jo Jack's replacement who was sent to Cherry school near Saigon, was killed yesterday by a truck running over him, it seems we cannot get a break.

We had been on the move for the better part of an hour, with wind and rain as our only companion.

I was on point; Baker filled the slack man's position, while Tate and Joseph covered our flanks and six. Coming into a flat clearing, we started up a small incline. It was then we heard a screams from an elephant in the distance. Stopping short, but then deciding to move closer, the cries grew louder.

In another twenty-minute's we stopped at a crevasse in the rocks by a large tree. Below us, we saw three natives working trying to free their elephant's foot from a hole. A large rock had rolled into the hole pinning the elephant there.

We were, told that the Jarai people were a primitive people. The Jarai diets included rice, vegetables, and fruits, and roots from certain plants. Their members often smoked pot rolled up in banana leaves. I wondered if this is where Donovan came up with the song, Mellow Yellow.

We had been so involved in watching the men trying to free the elephant; we failed to notice that two of the Jarai had simply walked up behind us, catching us unaware.

One of them spoke up. "Xin chào," (Hello) came from behind us in broken Vietnamese at best. As a group we turned, ready to fire!

Tate seemed to catch a few words of it. "Wait!" He said. "They mean us no harm!"

Joseph and I had rolled around the balls of our feet, weapons pointed with fingers on the triggers.

If they had wanted to harm us, we would have already been dead, I caught only a few words the man was saying as he, and Tate conversed.

"Tôi gián'.

"Did you get that?" Tate looking at me, "He said his name is Cockroach?"

"Cockroach can't be right." I said. "Tell him his new name is Chief, because he looks like a strong warrior!"

"CEF?" He stuttered.

"Chief," Tate corrected. "Chief," he said pointing to him, "Me soldier, you Chief!"

"Tôi Truong," (I Chief) he laughed.

The Chief and Tate talked for a spell, "He says he likes American soldiers, but the Vietcong and the NVA he does not like," Tate said. "They are speaking Austronesia, and Vietnamese mixed in."

I had no idea what, the hell Austronesia was, so I just shut up.

The chief continued talking, the more he talked the conversation slowed, once that happened I could understand him a lot better. I asked him if he had seen any activity north of where we were. He told us the Vietcong was gathering in an area east of his village. He believed they were looking for another way around the mountain other than Highway 19 to launch their attacks. Apparently, the area north of here suffered heavy bombing by the US opening areas of dense jungle heretofore. He said in order to get to where they were that we would have to go through his village to get there. I asked how long the Vietcong had been gathering, he said for the better part of a month. However, there were NVA coming across the DMZ from the north each week to meet the collecting Vietcong from the south.

We agreed to help them free the Chief's elephant, if he would let us follow him to his village where we would rest for the night before moving out early tomorrow morning. Shaking his head in agreement and smiling from ear to ear, he insisted we eat super with them, so we agreed.

Using a long pole the Chief's men helped cut from the forest, we carried it back to the elephant. We placed one end of the pole under the elephant's right foot and placed the short end on top of a large rock for advantage.

At that point, the four of us pulled down on the long end of the pole, and lifted the elephant's leg out of the hole. The giant held his foot in the air for a few minutes, and then with his handler guiding him, placed it on the ground. The leg seemed ok. The trainer had him bend a knee and climbed up on his back.

With the six-thousand pound gentle monster leading the way, the natives and our small band followed behind. The Chief walked with us talking mostly to SGT. Tate. We finally figured out his name. It was Tainan, not Cockroach. He liked the idea of being Chief Tainan accepted it once he learned the word Chief meant he was the leader.

He talked about the American Military base at Pleiku, saying that when he and his men did make contact with the soldiers there on occasion, how friendly they were to him and his people. He welcomed Americans because they gave his men „thuc pham (Food) and „kræka. (Crackers) Tainan spoke of his band of men killing the Vietcong when they came into their area. He was very unhappy with Ho Chí Minh for sending soldiers down from the north into their villages, killing his friends and neighbors.

It was late by the time we reached their village. Once there it was like walking onto a Johnny Weissmuller movie set. We expected Tarzan to swing in on a vine at any time. Their houses sat on stilts about five to six-feet above the ground to avoid flash floods...

They were very friendly and smiled a lot while welcoming us to their homes with opened arms, and invited us to share their food and shelter. They said the gods of the mountains wanted us there; our presence would bring them great blessings since we had helped with the elephant.

We settled in under a large square roof sitting on benches about two-feet off the ground. At least we were in the dry with a small fire for heat burning in the center of it all. They had a large pig roasting over the fire, I was especially thankful they were cooking it; I didn't care for raw pig.

A woman cut off large chunks of the meat making sure that we were, served first. We waited until everyone else was, served before we began eating. Another woman brought around a large pot of rice dipping it on our plates with her hand. In turn, we each said please and thank you. There was no silverware, so we as they ate with our fingers. Two children followed behind the woman giving us a large leaf to wipe our hands.

We only had a few chocolate bars, but we gave what we had to the Chief, telling him we thought the children would enjoy them. He had never tasted one before, and after doing so; he decided he would keep them for himself. We in no way offered to challenge his decision, whatever he wanted was fine with us.

The night passed without incident, our small team was up at daybreak and ready to move out. Each of us checked our weapons making sure they were loaded and ready to fire.

I enjoyed having dry feet for a change, even our boots had dried out somewhat in the night wind.

I kept looking for the elephants, there was more than one, I could hear them, but I couldn't see them. I thought they were magnificent animals.

Chief Tainan and three of his men met us at breakfast telling us they would show us where the Vietcong was located, Tate and I explaining to him how dangerous it could be for him and his men. Nevertheless, he insisted saying they had confronted the Vietcong on many an occasion over the years. After all, we were in the man's backyard. The fact was he managed to sneak up on us without any problems. It seemed to the Chief we needed him. Once again, we gave in.

After finishing eggs and homemade biscuits with a large glass of rice wine, we were on our way north. With the Chief and Baker on point, we followed about thirty-feet behind them. Tainan's men had brought bananas and mangos along. I ate two of the mangos, they were great, a first for me, but I promised myself I would have more in the future.

Joseph was lagging behind kissing and saying goodbye to two of the village girls. Seems he made new friends during the night.

Three-hours out of camp we had reached a point on the other side of the mountain where the Chief wanted to stop. He ordered two of his men to go farther north where they were and meet us on the other side. Their path would cover the northern area from in where the NVA had been coming in; the path would be a great deal easier to travel than the one the Chief had chosen for the rest of us.

The two men said their goodbyes, and wished us luck as they left.

The trees in this area were large, growing seemly out of the base of the large rocks protruding out of the side of the mountain. The area was teaming with wildlife. The birds were singing loudly as the monkeys seem to dance to their music, chattering and swinging from vine to vine. Our movements and noise seemed to go completely unnoticed by the wild life. Which meant they had gotten use to human's, mainly the NVA we were thinking.

Two hours later, we came to a flat knoll and decided to take a rest. We ate the rice we had in our packs with some leftover pork from the previous night's dinner. We caught water running out of a stream between the rocks boiling it using C-4 chunks as fuel. We let it boil for five minutes or longer to make sure we had removed the impurities before pouring into our canvass canteens. We repeated the steps until we had filled all of the bladder bags.

The Chief and his men laughed at us as they watched us, for they drank the water as is, and told us we were crazy, at least according to SGT. Tate.

On the move once again, we never stopped on the final four-hour leg of the journey. Other than taking brief breaks to relieve ourselves and then caught up with the others once we had.

Once we reached our meeting place, the Chief's men were already there. They had found more fruits along the way and offered us more mangos, and banana's. Seeking shelter under the trees from the rain, we drank tea and ate fruit for the next thirty-minutes or so. Break over;

we headed down the backside of the mountain toward where the Chief said the Vietcong was collecting. We were being cautious, more so than before. Charlie had a way of setting booby-traps in a trail; however, so far we had been lucky by not finding any. We wondered just what the, Vietcong were up to? My personal opinion was that they had considered this area as very safe for so long, they believed that no one knew that they were here. It would be a rare occurrence to catch them with their guard down; nevertheless, it appeared that we had.

Twenty- minutes later, we stopped again to regroup, the Vietcong were due south of us according to the Chief. We explained that we could take it from here, of course, he argued saying, and he and his men were not stopping. They would work their way east of the enemy where they would confront the Vietcong as they had before. Sitting us free to do what we wanted. They said goodbye to us as they trekked off down the side of the path disappearing in the heavy rain and fog.

"Shit," Baker spoke up. "Do you think they know what they are doing?"

"This is their backyard," I said. "They know this area a lot better than we do."

Joseph stepped up, "Why don't we work our way west and down? If we can get behind them, maybe, just maybe we can call in artillery strikes from a nearby Fire Base to help us take them out?"

Shaking my head no, "This is a Recon mission, we are not to make contact, remember?"

"I am with whatever we decide to do guys, although," Tate said. "I think just standing here is the wrong approach to the problem."

"I agree," Joe called it, "let's head west, and down!"

The rain was falling so hard you couldn't see five feet in front of us, but we moved west anyway using our hand-held compasses to guide our path only to stop a half hour later.

"This is no way to fight a goddamn war," Baker interjected. "Let's settle down for a little bit, see if this damn rain let's up. The last thing I want to do is walk up alongside Charlie by mistake."

We found a resting place and settled down for the long haul. I could not see the person seated next to me. Only thing I could hear was Baker complaining about the rain drops hurting his head when he was wringing the water out of his floppy hat.

Forty-five minutes passed before the deluge began to slack somewhat. It's still raining but at least it wasn't as hard as it was a few minutes ago. Again, we were up and moving due south this time. The forest floor was moving beneath us. The rain caused the dirt to turn into a mucky mud, conditions were miserable.

We hadn't assigned a point man as such; we had just come abreast of each other spreading out as we moved down the slippery slopes. We would stop occasionally checking the area below us with binoculars to see if we could see anything, so far, nothing.

In the faint distance and a half-hour later, we heard voices below us shouting out directions for everyone to help with the tents.

The runoff water from the mountainside had caused a flash flood that washed away everything in the encampment below. We spread out moving in for a closer look. It was the Vietcong all right; it appeared they had civilian prisoners with them, probably collecting them along the way. They had tied the villagers together placing them near trees on higher ground to keep them from being, washed away.

There was an area in front of them where two men and a woman lay dead. They were, apparently interrogating them, and then killing them one at a time. This made it our business; we were to intervene to help the civilian's if possible.

A high-ranking Vietcong Officer shouted out, "Đó là thoi gian đe bat đau Thr agai questing, mang lai cho cô!" (It's time to start the questioning again. Bring her!) He said pointing to a young girl.

Others were busily working on their lean-to's, trying to salvage what they could and move other tents away from the run offs.

We gathered quietly, I was the first to speak, "How many?"

"I would say a hundred or more," Tate offered. "Some could have been washed away; flash floods can be pretty intense."

They was a group of men down at the edge of the river bank calling out to others as if they were floating away or clinging on to something in the river below.

"About a hundred-thirty," Joseph said. "No more than that."

"Baker?" I asked.

"I agree with Joseph and Tate," he said, "A hundred to a hundred and thirty or so."

"What do we do about the prisoner's?" I asked.

"Nothing," Tate said. "It's time for us to do what we do. Let him continue to question the prisoner's; it could work to our advantage. I just hope it's enough of a diversion to work in our favor."

"Then let's do this." I offered.

Baker blandishing his knife, "Shouldn't, we wait for the Chief and his men to make the first move?"

"No we could lose the element of surprise," Tate said moving into position. "I am with Logan, let's get to it."

With the light fading, a gray fog had cut visibility to within thirty feet, which we would use for concealment. Our orders always including saving civilians when possible, so with that in mind, we began.

The Vietcong were so distracted and involved by doing what they could do to salvage their camp. They would never know we were there until it was too late. The plan was to encircle the camp taking out the stragglers on the outer edges of the circle first. Then work our way in.

We would work alone, so we divided ourselves moving off in different directions. I had selected the area just south of where they were questioning the villagers as my starting point. Getting into position, I moved into the shadows past the officer who was slapping the young woman in the face. He was asking her where the elders in her village had gone. With any answer she gave, he stuck her again. He had a growing audience as his men began grouping to witness the event.

I came upon a lone man trying to untangle his lean-to canvass from some tree limbs. Standing just inches away from him with his back to me. I waited until he stood up, grasped him by his chin with my left hand, aided by one quick motion, drove the blade up under the base of his sternum and up into his heart. Giving the blade a final twist, his body stiffened for a few brief seconds before going limp. I let him down gently into the mud soaked ground and walked away wiping blood on my trousers.

Moving back into the shadows, I repeated the process about twenty more times until I came to a clearing and stopped. Up the hill in front of me, I spotted the Chief and his men busy doing as we had done.

Without warming, I thought someone had discovered us, or one of the Chief's men. Someone had fired a single shot from an AK. Responding by moving toward the shot, I saw a Vietcong who had just shot at a deer.

"Hôm nay, chúng ta ăn huou!" (Today, we eat deer!) He said proudly. "Cai! Giúp anh ta voi thân thit cua!" (Come! Help with the carcass.)

We stepped back into the shadows where we began anew our deadly mission; the rain, fog, and darkness were indeed our friends this day.

With two more down, I began working my way back to where the officer was questioning another prisoner. The woman whom he had been questioning on my first pass, lay dead at his feet, he had slit her throat.

We had encircled the entire camp in less than an hour. We had killed them all except for the deer hunter and the thirty or so watching the officer torturing his current suspect.

We walked up behind them without so much as a notice, "Dung lai!" (Stop!) I screamed.

Some of the Vietcong reached for their weapons, the Chief's men opened fire killing them where they stood. The rest of them and another officer thrust their hands high above their heads surrendering. Baker ordered them to get down in the mud on their faces. Joseph and two of the Chief's men went about relieving them of their weapons.

I walked into the circle where the officer stood; he wore the rank of, Captain, "Dee wee, anh co noi duroc tieng Anh không?" (Captain, do you speak English?)

"Không! (No!)

With my K-9 pointing at his head, and his hands high in the air, I walked up to him grabbing his shoulder, and then turned his back to me. I removed his pistol from its holster tossing it into the mud a few feet away, and searched him for any other weapons.

Joseph stepped in freeing the man the Captain had been questioning.

"Tie this ass-fuck to that log," I ordered.

Joe responded by doing just that. Once he had the asshole laced to that log, he stepped away.

"Hãy xem làm the nào ban thích nó?"

I stepped in, (Let's see how you like it?)

With my forefinger pointing, I moved it toward his forehead. He did everything he could to avoid my touch; he didn't want to lose his spirit.

"Xin vui lòng không có không có không có!" (N0 N0 NO Please!).

Grabbing him by the hair and with him squirming, I touched him on his temple several times with my forefinger. "Anh co khoe không bay tôi gio, du mi ami?" (Do you understand me now, motherfucker?)

"Có!" (Yes!) It was plain to see fear had replaced his arrogance.

One of the captured villagers got up, walked over to me as if she was out for a stroll. Then picked up the Captain's pistol from the mud, "He killed my sister," she said speaking perfect English. "I would shame my ancestors if I did not avenge her death," staring at me as if asking my permission.

I took a step backwards giving her my approval; she spit in his face, and then pressed the muzzle of the weapon into the Captain's temple. "He has no honor; he must die like a pig!" With that, she shot him once in the side of the head watching as his body bolted violently back and forth before going limp and falling into the mud. Then she stepped over his body, and emptied the pistol into his face. She turned around, looking back at me. "Now he is a dead pig with no honor. May his spirit roam the heavens forever," she said throwing the pistol back into the mud.

"Are you ok?" I asked.

"Yes, we all are ok now. My name is, Ha`ng, Sergeant Logan," she said looking at my nametag.

The word Ha`ng meant, Angel in the Full Moon. "Ha`ng is a beautiful name."

"Thank you."

Looking around, I realized Tate wasn't with us. "Where's Tate?"

No one had seen him, so Baker and I went looking for him.

Joseph stayed behind to take charge of the prisoners. Together, Joe and our newfound friends stood guard over the Vietcong while Baker and I went to look for Tate.

Freed, the captured villagers had already begun scrounging for food as they gleaned the dead for weapons and documents.

After fifteen minutes of looking in every direction, Baker remembered where he had lost sight of Tate, he yelled out, "SGT. Tate!" A short time later, "Over here," Baker, cried out. "Over here!"

As I moved in, I saw Tate lying in the mud on his back. Reaching his side, I could see he is still alive but his vitals were very weak. Baker gave him a shot of Morphine as I examined the wound. The round had entered just below his right nipple, and probably punctured a lung as well. All I knew was that we had to get him out of there.

Baker, searched for Tate's medical kit, for it had the Hespan in it in case we needed it.

Finally retrieving the field radio from the top of the hill, I radioed command detailing our situation, and location. Asking for an immediate MEDAVAC extraction for Tate, I also requested claymores and C-4. We were going to leave some surprises for Charlie.

While waiting, we made Tate as comfortable as possible. Ha`ng, the Vietnamese woman made her way up to where we were. "Please, maybe I can help him," she said dropping to her knees beside Tate, the muddy water splashing all over her.

"The man who had shot the deer must have hit him. There was only one shot," saying as I watched the young woman work.

"Thank God, he did not yell out," Baker said.

"He wouldn't have done that."

"The bullet did not go through; it is still in there," her face filled with sadness. "I am afraid I can be of no help."

"We have help coming," I said, "but thank you for trying."

We left Tate lying in the mud just as we had found him; I didn't want to move him fearing the bullet could cause more damage.

"Miss Ha`ng, we can take you and the others to Saigon if you wish," shifting the weight of the radio to my other shoulder. "They have people there who can help you and your people."

"No thank you. We will return to our village," wiping her face. "We will be ok."

"Are you sure?"

"Yes," pointing, "The Captain is dead. As I have said, we will be ok."

I had a thousand questions for her running through my mind, but the Huey's were arriving in the near distance.

On the ground and shown, the way, the medics scrambled up the hillside to where we were standing, then they went about carrying Tate back toward the waiting helicopter.

Baker and I went back to where the villagers had put all of the documents they had taken from the Vietcong, alive or dead. Unbeknown to us, Ha`ng had gotten to the documents before us.

Then we went to the, Huey's, where we unloaded the explosives we had requested.

The Chief and his men gathered around us watching. They stood proudly telling us that it had been a pleasure fighting alongside us today. We thanked him, telling him he was welcome to fight with us anytime. He was very pleased with himself over the fact that his men were as good as we were. Then he began passing around a flask of Banana and Rice Rum that he had taken from a Vietcong. He asked what we were doing with the explosives, so we filled him in. He said he and his men would help us place them; they didn't want to come back this way maybe finding them by mistake.

They had sent in three helicopters of Marines to load up the captured Vietcong. They were tying their hands and feet together, preparing to load them into the choppers by the time we got back to them.

There were two-Australians dressed in nondescript uniforms, no insignia's, no stripes, or bars, no nametags. There was nothing to identify them.

Walking up to one of the Marines, "Who's in charge?" I asked.

"I am, SGT. Withers," spoke up.

Nodding, "Who are they?"

"Assholes," said Withers, "CIA Mother-fuckers! I'd say!"

"And their function?"

"To fuck up everything they touch if you want my opinion."

"Is there a problem, Mate?" One of them said noting that we were talking about them as they came abreast of us.

"No problem, just wondering who's actually taking charge of the prisoner's for my AAR report."

"Sergeant Logan, is it?" As his partner joined us, "Let's just say you are the first, you are Sergeant Logan One, I'm Sergeant Logan Two, and my friend here is Sergeant Logan Three. You have no need to know who we are. Let it suffice to say we are Charlie's worst nightmare, and your best friend." He said. "You do not want to know what we do or how we do it. Is that clear?"

I smiled at him.

"We'll be on our way. I suggest you carry on with your rescuing attempts of which I am sure no one will ever give a real shit, other than yourself and your young lady friend over there."

"Just following orders."

"Of course you are."

Ha`ng came to my side, folding her right arm into mine. "It's time for us to go," she said pulling at me.

The Marine's yelled that they were loaded and ready to roll, the two Aussies turned and walked away.

"You don't want to mess with them," Ha`ng said letting go of my hand as if she knew them. "They kill for no reason."

The medics put Tate on the helicopter with three of the injured villagers and took flight.

Baker had picked up all of the remaining papers stuffing them into a bag he had found. He stored them in a cave of sorts; one that Charlie had dug in the side of a hill to store food in.

One of the women we had rescued went about making dinner for all of us. As the Chief had ordered his men to stand guard, Baker went with them.

I found a flat rock and decided to let the matter drop concerning the two Australians. Taking a seat, I decided to wait for something to eat.

Minutes later, Ha`ng stepped up. "Would you like some tea?"

"Thank you," I said taking the cup from her as she sat next to me. "Want a candy bar?"

"No, thank you," touching me on the arm, "Thank you and your men for helping us."

"May I tell you something?"

"Of course", she said taking a sip of tea.

"I have to tell you about your sister."

Her eyes narrowing, "What?"

"As we were moving into position, I saw what the Captain was doing to her, but there was nothing I could do at the moment to save her, I'm sorry."

"We are appointed once to die, each in our on time, it was her time, it's not your fault," with tears in her eyes. "I can only thank you for the lives you and your men did save."

I pulled her into me giving her a hug of reassurance. "How are you going to get home?

She gave me a quick hug and then let go. "We will be alright. Our village is less than ten-miles away; we will leave in the morning before you place the explosives."

Brushing a leaf from her hair, "While in captivity, did the Captain or his men say anything that may be useful to us?"

"Nothing that would be of any use," she said. "They only wanted the girls and boys to take with them. They questioned our old people asking them for money, and other valuables."

We were up and moving before daylight. I had only seen Ha`ng covered with mud and blood last night. This morning she had taken a bath at the river, and was wearing clean clothes now. Having the opportunely to look at her more closely, I found her to be very striking. I was surprised her captives hadn't raped or even killed her.

The villagers had buried their dead; they were standing over the graves saying prayers for their departed spirits. Others were already filing out of the camp heading back to their village, leaving the gravesites behind.

Ha`ng left with a hand full of others who carried their belongings across their backs and atop their heads, and following the main group.

The Chief and his men had gathered with us to eat and drink, the Chief finishing the last of the rice wine.

We grabbed our gear, Baker carrying the radio left me to bring the claymores. Joseph and the pair of the Chief's men carried the rest of the explosives. As we moved up the hill setting the traps, the villagers got further and further away until they were finally out of sight.

Our task completed, Baker called for Peaches and Jewels to pick us up. We thanked the Chief and his men for their help and then departed as friends. With a wish that one day, we would meet again.

James Lovell and Buzz Aldrin splash down
In Gemini 12 which concludes the last
Gemini mission.
11/15/66
UPI Radio
Taken from a rebroadcast radio
Program on 12/30/66, never heard
The original news when it happened.
It made me proud to be an American.

CHAPTER FIFTEEN

MEETING MAYA'S MOTHER: Long Binh was as busy as ever. Her Mother lived on base in civilian quarters that housed all the indigenous personnel. She had a job cleaning the officers' quarters as well as their individual offices within the base. According to Maya, she worked from, eight in the morning until five in the afternoon. She's due home anytime, so we decided to have tea while we waited. While waiting, Maya gave me a short tour through the small spotless apartment. It's furnished with the standard military furniture, which came with all of the apartments. Much like the one, Joseph and I shared while living with the military police, beige rugs, with matching drapes over the windows.

With an hour and a half to kill, Maya and I stood in the doorway of her bedroom, and began making out. She pushed me back against the open door and kissed me. Of course, I kissed her back. She moved further down and unzipped my trousers…

An hour or so later, we moved to the kitchen table and had some tea while we waited for her mother. Maya had to go to the bathroom so I had more tea.

I had gone to see Reyna this morning before Maya and I left. I wanted to tell her that I wanted to see if we could work things out between us, but she wasn't there. Dr. Drake told me she had left for Long Binh earlier this morning to pick up some medical supplies, instead of waiting for the regular supply chopper. Then I found out from Maya that Reyna was meeting us here about four-thirty so we could help her take the supplies back to our camp. I hoped she would get here soon, helping Reyna would provide us with a good excuse to leave.

"Hi," the Mother said entering though the front door closing it behind her. Walking over to me, she offered her hand. "Nice to meet you Sergeant Logan, I have heard so much about you."

"Good to meet you as well," I said, shaking her hand. I waited until she removed her coat, piling it onto a chair in the hall. "I hope you don't mind I brought you a gift?"

She smiled, opening the package; she removed three homemade patch quilts from back home. "You may call me, Miss Long," she said looking at me. Then almost immediately turned her attention back to the gift, "Oh, these are beautiful!" She exclaimed. "Where in the world did you ever find something like this?"

I was amazed at how well she spoke English, trying to be nice. "Miss Long, my grandmother and her church group made those by hand, I asked her to send them to me as a gift for you and Maya."

"There are three blankets, but I only have two beds," she laughed. "There is only Maya and myself."

Long looked thirty, but Maya had told me she was forty. Yet, she's in great shape; her body is nice and tight. Her completion except for a few slight wrinkles matched Maya's. She was a very handsome woman. "I also had one made for your ancestors," I said. "I know when you give a gift; you should always provide another one for such a purpose."

She placed them one by one on the sofa, "We follow some traditions," bending over at the waist, "but we are not traditional by any means," saying as she turn and joined Maya at the table. She sat between Maya and me pouring, herself a cup of tea. "My daughter tells me you wanted to ask for her hand in marriage?" She mused. "I assume she also told you of her impending marriage to, Master Chien?" Translated into (To Battle or Fight).

"She has."

Turning to Maya, "Please let the Sergeant and I speak alone."

Maya got up, looking back as she walked away; she went to her bedroom at the end of the hall and closed the door.

Long turning back to me, "What I'm about to tell you will remain with us if you care for the safety of my daughter, Sergeant," her senses heightened.

"Of course."

"Years ago, I married a Vietcong high-ranking official, Maya's father. It was most unfortunate, but he beat me. I schooled myself in English, I had hoped to escape to America, but Long Binh was as far as I managed to get. Three years later, my husband was, killed. You must understand that Maya is the best thing that ever happened in my life, she is my life," she offered.

"It was Master Chine's father who attended to our safe transport, his son and Maya is of the same age. I promised Master Chien the gift of Maya as his son's wife in payment for his kindness. Surely, you can see my promise to him must be honored?"

I had to ask. "Master Chine's father is, Vietcong?"

"Yes, he is."

"And the son, Chien, he is Vietcong?"

"Yes."

"There is nothing I can do or say to change your mind?"

Long, shaking her head, "No."

"What about what Maya wants?"

"My daughter wants what will make her mother happy. Her feelings for you will pass. She is still young so she will soon learn that being a woman means responsibility to family and honor. That over shadows everything else. Maya will be a good wife. She will be standing behind a man who will help lead Vietnam to its victory over the Americans," she boasted. "As far as you are concerned, she will never stand behind a blood thirsty American soldier who lives to kill and murder with no forethought."

"Well, seems we know each other. You come down on the side of the Vietcong, who kills women; children and the old...take the young boys from their villages to suit your purposes." Long, in Vietnamese meant Dragon, the name suited her. We could spend the rest of the evening complementing each other, but the truth was I wanted to reach out and punch the Bitch's ticket.

"I expect you to be shocked, Sergeant. I also know you will struggle within yourself over the knowledge you have just learned. Maybe even turn me into the authorities?" Her eyes narrowing, threaten. "I am counting on the love that you have for my daughter not to do that. You see, if anything happens to me, they will take her away and torture Maya for having sexual relations with an American soldier. A soldier that she let take her virtue," Smiling and confident, she took another sip of tea. "They will kill her and throw her body into a hole and burn it like so much trash."

"You must know I could take your life right now, and then Maya would be free to go with me."

"You think my daughter would go with you if you killed her, mother?" She laughed. "You have seen how obedient she is to her mother. I speak, she moves. She would not go anywhere with you. Maya would not shame me. Nor disgrace herself or her family in order to please you."

Maya came down the hall screaming! "Yes I would! Mother, is wrong!" Upset and crying. "I hate you!"

Long got up going straight for Maya, as she did, I grabbed Long by the hair and slammed her face into the wall. She fell to the floor unconscious.

Maya stood over her crying. "I must kill my mother!"

Holding to Maya, "She can't stop us, I won't let her," I promised.

"You not thinking, she knows people who can find us, think of SGT. Savage! His secret place will be found!"

I grabbed her by the arm. "Let's just get out of here."

"No," Maya becoming hysterical. "She must die! We must take her to the Major!" She said, running off into her mother's bedroom only to return carrying a stack of military forms. "Here! You see for self."

Studying the forms, I saw orders to almost every military combat unit operating in the South East Asian Theater. While cleaning the Officers Quarter's and the Offices on the base. Long had been gathering intelligence, and furnishing the Intel to the Vietcong and NVA. These orders were dated back only for a week.

"How long has your mother worked here on the base?"

"A little over a year."

"How long has she been collecting information?"

"Same amount of time."

"Has she asked you to help her?"

"Yes."

"And did you?"

"No."

"What did she ask you to do?"

"She wanted me to question the wounded soldier's at the hospital, find out their company's strength, their locations, and report back to her."

"And you never did that for her, not even once?"

"Jack! In the hospital, did I ever ask you or Hocus, any questions about your business?"

"No."

SGT. Savage's compound is safe! I would never give her information. I hate what the Vietcong do. They make me sick! I would never be on their side, I would rather be dead!"

Taking her into my arms, I kissed the top of her head, "Calm down dear, I had to ask."

She pulled away, her gaze meeting mine. "We must go!"

"We need to get her into the car without drawing attention to ourselves; can you drive it into the garage?"

"Yes," as she went out to move the car.

I called the Officer's Bar at the airport, "Teddy here," on the other end.

"Is Peaches there, please?"

"Just a minute!"

Long started to come around, getting to her knees, I carried the phone over to her, using the base of the phone, I smashed her in the back of the head, and she went out like a light.

"Hello!"

Placing the receiver to my ear, "Peaches?"

"Yeah buddy I'm here."

"We need an emergency extraction out of here. It's imperative that we get back to camp right away."

"Sure, I'll be waiting."

We are going to have a passenger on the way back."

"Ten-Four!"

I placed the handset back into its cradle as Maya emerged from the garage. "Ready," she said.

"You have a nurse's uniform here?"

"Yes!"

"Put it on."

"But, why?"

"Just put it on."

"Ok," she said speeding off.

I picked up Long, and carried her out to the car, once there. I placed her into the back seat, and then got back there with her.

Maya came out of the house straightening her hat and climbing in; she started the car and backed out of the garage. We were finally on the move. As we approached the main gate I put Long's head into my lap holding her hand as if she was performing oral sex.

Luckily, the car had a military sticker on the front bumper, as we approached the gate; an MP stopped us while he went about checking the bumper sticker. Looked at Maya for a moment, and then went about inspecting the back seat. I moved my fingers through Long's hair as if we were lovers.

He looked at me and me at him; I winked and looked down at her. Opening the gate, he gave me a smile with two thumbs up as he motioned us through.

Once at the helicopter, Long woke up again, looking around recognizing where she was. "You will never get away with this;" she said firmly. "I am not getting on that helicopter!"

I grabbed her putting her into a chokehold, in a matter of seconds she passed out. I carried her in my arms with Maya following in her nurse's uniform. Making it appear that we were taking a patient aboard the, Huey.

Peaches took us up and away. With Maya's help, we used the seat belts to tie the bitch to the seat, and without the protection of a Flak Jacket under her narrow ass.

Back at camp, Maya and I took what information we had to the Major; in turn, he contacted the Provost Marshall's Office in Saigon. They were to stake out Long's home in case anyone showed up for any more paperwork. They were to look out for Reyna as well and get her the hell out of there.

"Is she acting on her own?" Baginski asked chewing on a cigar.

"She had others who cleaned and cooked and gave her important papers also," Maya twisting a tissue in her hands. "I only know one name, she works for Colonel Smith, I do not know where he works, but her name is, Miss Phuong."

Taking the cigar out of his mouth, he lit it. "Can you tell us what she looks like?"

"She is older lady, has thinning hair, is very polite, and uses her manners to help hide her real identity."

"Okay. I will get this information to the right people. Until then, can you return to your nurses duties? Lt. Hawks not being here has left us short-handed."

"Yes Sir, I will go now, thank you, Sir."

I walked Maya outside and gave her a kiss goodbye. Baginski met me. "Let's get a cup of coffee."

"Yessir," as we headed for the mess hall. "What are we going to do with Miss Long, Sergeant?"

"Kill her and dump her ass over a cliff. Who cares?"

"A bit overboard, don't you think, Sergeant? However, I will say that your hearts in the right place," Baginski sucking on his cigar.

We stopped. "Sir, if we turn her over for questioning, any spying Vietcong Agent worth his salt will get wind

245

of it. That will compromise our security here. It's an unacceptable risk."

"I'm not comfortable with us killing her; I'm still getting dissension over Agent White's death. I would rather turn her over to someone else."

"Who Sir? If Long is turned over to anyone else, we could lose her. She's a well-spoken person. If she convinces someone to let her go, she wouldn't think twice about condoning the killing of her daughter or us for that matter. And that's a definite possibility."

"Can you do it?" Baginski asked. "I mean kill her?"

"I could, but had rather not, Peaches said to talk to SGT. Savage about it." We turned walking toward the mess hall again. "He said Savage would know how to handle it."

"She's in the stockade now?"

"Yessir."

"Let's keep a close eye on her until Higgins and Savage gets back tomorrow."

"Yessir."

A guard from the stockade approaching, "Major Baginski," he called out. Again we stopped. "Sir, the Long woman passed out in her cell, her head wound is still bleeding. We took her to the M*A*S*H Unit, they think she may have a concussion!"

"What is being done for security? This woman is Vietcong Sergeant."

"We have two men on her, Sir."

"Thank you Sergeant, I want two men on her twenty-four hours a day! That means at all times, Sergeant. Understand?"

"Yes Sir, I will see to it."

"Thank you Sergeant."

"Yes Sir," he said leaving.

We went to the mess hall and had chow. Baker and Joseph came in later. When the Major left, I joined them at their table. Filling them in on what had happened while having a large slice of apple pie and some more chocolate milk. We talked for a while, Baker told me SGT Tate was awake and was asking for me, and that he and Joseph had spent the morning visiting him, so I decided I would visit him later.

It was after six by the time I got to the hospital. Walking in, I spotted a nurse coming toward me. "Excuse me, could you tell me which bed, SGT. Tate is in?"

"Around the corner," pointing, "First bed on the left."

"Thank you," I said following her directions.

"Jack!" Tate smiled. "Glad to see you, buddy!"

Setting next to him, I shook his hand, "Glad to see you too," smiling back.

"I didn't think I was going to make this one," Tate added.

I retrieved a couple of chocolate bars from my pocket. "I brought these just for you; I know how you like`em."

"Thanks Jack, you're a good man," he said, laying them atop his nightstand, his demeanor turning serious. "Thank you for saving my ass back there."

"Wasn't just me buddy, Baker and the Vietnamese girl Ha`ng were there too. The girl did what she could for you. I'm just glad you are ok." I stood up, grabbed a pillow from the empty bed next to him placing it onto the seat of the chair. "These chairs are like sitting on a goddamn rock," as I sat back down again, my ass settling into the pillow's softness. "Awww, that's better."

"I got a letter from my wife today," he said, picking it up removing a photo from the envelope. "Our daughter had a birthday last Monday, here's her picture," handing it to me.

The photo was of a pretty, blonde-haired girl in her teens, others of the same age bracketed her in the background. "How old is she?"

"Seventeen."

"She's pretty; the girl is going to be a heartbreaker."

"That's her sister Elaine behind her on the left, she is nineteen."

"Very pretty girls."

"That's Dan on the right, the oldest; he's twenty-two, a Navy man of all things."

"I hope he's not anywhere near this place."

"No, they stationed him in Norfolk; he will finish out his time there, then he's going to college to become a lawyer. I am a proud father as well as a proud husband. I cannot wait to get back to her and the rest of the family."

"I grew up in Norfolk, my old man worked in the shipyard there."

He laughed. "Like they say, it's a small world."

"You said you can't wait to get back to her, are you leaving the Army?"

"No way, I am only five years away from my thirty; it's going to be your mission to keep me alive until then."

"Tell yah what, Sarge, you cover my young ass, and I will cover your old ass."

"You got it bud;" he said setting up on the edge of the bed. "I have to drain my lizard, I will be right back."

"I'll walk with you; I'm looking for Maya anyway. We arrested her mother today."

"For what?" He said looking surprised.

"Spying."

"No shit?"

As we walked down the hall toward the latrine I spotted Maya at the nurse's station; I stayed there while Tate went to the latrine, "How are you doing?" I asked taking her into my arms.

Looking up at me, "I ok," she said giving me a quick kiss. "We are busy; two of the four teams sent out this morning were hit. We may lose a couple men."

I saw two guards stationed at the other end of the hallway. "Is your mother over there?" I pointed.

Looking in that direction, "Yes, it is time I check on her. Did you speak with the Major about her? Will they execute her?"

"We will talk about it later. Has Reyna returned yet?"

"No, I worry about her; we need her on the floor."

I gave her another quick kiss, Tate is returning from the latrine. "I will see you later," my hand on her face as I left.

"Ok," as she walked away looking at me back over her shoulder.

Tate and I came along a side of each other while going back to his area.

"She is a pretty one, Logan, which one have you decided on, or have you?"

"Which one?"

"C'mon buddy, we all know. It must be tearing you apart, choosing between Reyna and Maya. I sure as hell wouldn't want to choose."

"It's killing me to be honest."

Just then, four shots from a .45 rang out across the ward. Turning around, I only saw one guard standing. The nurses over there began screaming and running over one another in an attempt to get out of there. Adding to the commotion, five more shots echoed across the large room, the remaining guard went down. Running down the hall toward the scene of the shooting, I saw Long standing with the pistol in her right hand. I drew my weapon from its holster, clicking off the safety. When I got there, I saw blood all over the floor and walls; all three, both guards and Maya were down.

"OH God NO!" I screamed.

Long fired the pistol's final shot hitting the wall behind me! She was out of ammo! Walking at a rapid pace, I went straight for her. She went for the dead guard's pistol lying on the floor at the foot of the second bed where he had dropped it. I never missed a step nor did I hesitate. I fired four rapid shots at her head with three of the bullets hitting their mark. Long's body lunged backwards and slid up against the wall before stopping. Still walking, I fired four more rounds into her chest. The Dragon Lady was dead! She lay in a pool of blood sprawled out on the floor.

Turning I saw Maya on the floor with half of her face blown away in a gathering pool of blood. On the way to her I dropped the pistol and fell to my knees as I reached her body. I pulled her head and upper torso up into my arms. Her blood streamed down over my hands and my right arm. Holding her to my chest, I felt her heart as it slowed and finally made its last faint beat; I cried uncontrollably as I rocked her body back and forth kissing what was left of her face. I held her tightly in my arms refusing to let go. Asking myself why God would let such a sweet pure of heart person such as she was to just die, and for what purpose? Then I realized it wasn't God that failed her, it was me. I had failed to keep her safe, failed her in so many ways.

* * * *

Two Days Later

Major Baginski thought it best to end it here, instead of sending Long's body back to Long Binh for burial. He and SGT. Savage had her body put into the unmarked section in the back northeast corner of the compound's cemetery. The Major wanted no questions coming from command, which would require a lot of explaining. He filed a report. Stating that Long was drowned in the river below the compound while trying to escape, adding that her body was never recovered.

We had a closed casket ceremony for Maya. There were photos of remembrance at the gravesite for the taking. One of the Doctors was heavy into photography; he had taken endless pictures of everyone working in the hospital at one time or another, including the patients. One in particularly caught my attention, it had been taken the first day I had seen her. She was wearing her nurse's uniform without her hat. I remembered her taking it off as her shift ended. Her long flowing hair down her back, she was smiling as she held a medical tray in her right hand with a carton of milk meant for me. She had her right forefinger pushing her long straight hair back over her ear with her left hand. It was the same morning as I had awakened from surgery. I took two of the photos for myself.

Maya had made many friends and had touched many hearts; she was a sweet gentle soul. Her spirit would surely live for as long as we remembered her.

They laid her to rest in the front section near the M*A*S*H Unit. Its Savages equivalent to our Arlington National Cemetery, Savage referred to everyone buried there as his children. It was complete with miniature white headstones and numbers instead of names. The words Heavens Alter carved into the stonework that supported the arch at the front of the cemetery. A golden Buddha sat in the middle surrounded by a circled fountain and pool, a very classy place of rest for the departed souls.

They placed Maya into a body bag then placed it into a wooden coffin hand crafted by Savages people. Before they sealed the coffin, I placed fifty White Orchids over the body bag. The Orchid (The Queen of The World of Flowers) was her favorite. I wanted to bring her Cherry Blossoms flowers, which were the meaning of her name; however, I was unable to find any.

Numb, I stood watching as they went about filling the grave with dirt. By this time, almost everyone else had left. Savage was talking to me, but I could not hear him.

"Sergeant Logan!" Savage repeated.

Finally breaking through, I turned to him.

"I need her full name for my records."

"I can't tell you," remembering what Maya and I had talked about the first day we met. "It's just, Maya."

Savage thought about it for a moment. "Then Mate, Maya it is."

I stopped writing about anything to do with the funeral, I ask you to forgive me, and I know it's abrupt and short. Know to that nothing is missing it is just not written. I decided to keep what I had for Maya in my heart instead of sharing it with others. Not out of selfishness, but out of respect for, Maya. If these notes are, found. Just know that a piece of me died on this day. I have no idea how many pieces I have left before I meet God.

*The US Aircraft Carrier Oriskany nicknamed
The Mighty O suffered from a magnesium
flare. That was accidentally ignited resulting
in a fire killing forty-four men in August in the
Gulf of Tonkin. The boat is under-going
Repairs this month, and will return to
service very soon.
12/30/66*

CHAPTER SIXTEEN

0830 OPERATION CENTER: MISSION MA2235
RESCUE: Sông Cuu Long. (River of Nine Dragons),
12/30/66. Major Baginski had ordered our team to immediate alert. Something big was in the works.

Thoughts of Maya were coursing through my brain
when ordered to come to Operation Room immediately.
Word was Lt. Higgins was to be Squad Leader on the
mission and that was fine with me; I would trust the man
with my life any day of the week.

First Lt. Mason made an excellent speaker since
assigned to the unit as our Operations Officer.

"Gentlemen," he started. "We just received word that one of our officer's has been captured. It happened at Long Binh four days ago. Lt. Reyna Hawks has been taken by Vietcong to an area in Sông Cuu Long," he said. "One of our allies, a New Zealand force operating in the area reports seeing an American woman matching Nurse Hawks' description. She was, seen at Suet Crossing, two-miles south of Sông Cuu Long. They have men stationed there on a mop up mission," he added. "The team leaves within the hour, Sergeant's Logan, Tate, Sacks, and Baker, will make up the rescue team with Lt. Higgins as SL." He said, clearing his throat. "SSgt Tate will be Team Leader. In order to have surprise on our side this will be a LALO (Low Altitude Low Operation) parachute drop. Your ceiling will be seventy-six meters or two-hundred-and-fifty-feet respectfully. Peaches will deploy. Major Baginski apologizes for his absence, but he wishes you luck, and God speed."

"Logan?" Baker said.

I turned to him but my mind was elsewhere.

"I have been calling you for ten minutes!" Looking at me, "Hey, you ok?"

"Yeah," I said standing up, "I'm ok. Let's go."

On our way to the chopper, Joseph joined us. "Man," he said. "When and where did they capture her?"

"Had to be at Maya's mother's house, we knew she would be stopping by to get a ride back here with us. She was picking up medical supplies for the camp."

"If you knew she was coming there, why didn't you wait for her?"

"Good goddamn question. We should have waited for Reyna. I thought she would just knock and not getting an answer, she'd just leave and come back here."

We stopped just long enough to get our packs and weapons from the barracks, and then reported to the helicopter pad. Peaches had already loaded our chutes, all we had left to do, was put them on once airborne. We passed out some prepared food we had collected from the mess hall, died fish and brown rice being at the top of the list. Baker and Joseph had brought two large packs of beef jerky.

At hundred-and-ten-knots and two-hundred-fifty-feet above the target area, the rice paddies and bushes below us were nothing more than a blur.

The Drop Zone was approaching fast, by Peaches pushing forward on the cyclic-stick the nose of the Huey went down. Two of us at a time readied ourselves, one on the right and one of the left jumped in counts of five until all of us were out of the chopper. Because of the shifting and swirling winds, we could end up anywhere. I hoped landing not too far from the rendezvous point.

Unfortunately, on my way down, the ground was so black I couldn't see anything; I prayed that a tree would not pop up in front of me. At my young age, I didn't need a Colonoscopy, giving a completely new meaning to here comes the Choo-Choo.

The wind rushed by, and then, splat! I hit a rice paddy, and landed navel deep in slime. I finally managed to get the parachute and harness off. Knowing I had to conceal it. I began making my way out of there. I could hear the Huey's sound fading in the distance wishing I were on board; at least I'd be dry. Moving through the mud had quickly drained my strength. It was all I could do to pull myself through the mud, but I knew I had to do it. The process happened only by inches at a time. Stopping and starting repeatedly. Seems as if it took me an hour to go thirty-feet, but I finally made it. Reaching the edge of the paddy, I hid the chute and harness in the mud and weeds.

I had the Green Eye protected with plastic covering in my rucksack; I abruptly removed it and began searching the immediate area around me. Looking for any signs of the enemy and/or my team, I had guessed they were already at the meeting place by now. I knew they would only wait thirty-minutes for me to catch up before they started out on their own. I rested a few more minutes then began moving out, using the compass on the wristwatch that Reyna gave me. My K-9 was mud soaked from the stock up to the end of the firing chamber. As I walked, I tried cleaning it off as much as possible. Moving, my strength slowly began to return, as a result I picked up the pace.

They often referred to the maps of Vietnam as *'Comic Books'* because they were so complicated making them a joke to read. Every hill, every valley, every road, every color you could think of, reds, blues, and a shit load of various greens on twenty-five pound weight, paper.

As I stopped and checked my position, I heard someone or something to my far right. Going down on one knee looking through the night scope, I spotted a tall figure moving in the same direction as I. He was walking with a limp; it had to be either Higgins or Tate, since they were the tallest members of the team. Not wanting to yell out, I injected a shell into the chamber of my K-9. The figure heard me and stopped, using his scope, he spotted me, and we began walking toward each other.

It was Higgins. In a low voice, "What happened to you?" Seeing me, mud soaked.

"I ended up in a fuckin' rice paddy."

"Me too," Higgins said pointing to his knee, "I landed on a rock! Hate to cut this short, but are you ready?"

"Let's go," I offered.

Together we moved in a straight line. Shortly after and using the scope we found the others in the distance.

Ten minutes later, Higgins asked, placing his equipment on the ground and dropping his trousers. "Anyone hurt besides me?"

Baker stepped up looking at Higgins knee. "Lieutenant, let me look at that for you." Getting down on one knee, Baker held a small flashlight with a red night vision plate over the lens. The flashlight gave off a faint red-glow, but you could clearly see the deep gash just above the knee joint.

"We have to stitch that," Joseph said. "It's probably infected already." Taking a small bottle of peroxide from his kit, he poured the liquid into the wound washing the debris out of the cut. Watching it foam before putting it away.

Baker pushed the air out of a prepackaged Novocain syringe, and then stabbed the needle into the edge of the wound in two places in order to numb it.

Quietly as possible, "Jesus Christ, feels like you are using a goddamn nail!"

It was all we could do not to laugh. Baker waited until the wound was numb before he sat about stitching it.

Tate and I stood guard; there wasn't anything out there other than gathering rain clouds in the distance. Lighting flashed over a large hill beyond us, we could smell the rain coming.

"Let's get out of here," Higgins ordered pulling up his pants.

We headed northeast in a single column, Baker, taking point. As always, I was right behind him in the Slack position. After traveling about forty-five minutes or so, we approached a tree line, once there we stopped.

Baker was the first to spot them, using hand signals. He motioned to area forty-feet in front of us, signaling that there were two guards. Using the night scope, they stood out like green Easter Eggs, one asleep, the other one stood leaning against a tree eating something out of his right hand. I had a feeling this would be the first of many to come. We were getting close to the village, so we separated. It was each man for himself. It would be daylight soon so we had to move. Baker and Joe went to take out the two guards.

Higgins ordered me, and Tate to go with him to the next point of entry into the village. We left the others to their duties as we made our way south approaching the village away from the main road. The road would be laden with booby-traps and mines. I went for the area less traveled with Higgins and Tate in tow. Letting the night vision scope guide my path as we went, wasn't long before we reached the wire surrounding the village; we were approaching the latrine area in the back corner of the village. The smell of shit was unmistakable, but the safest approach by far. In all of the missions we had ever done, there had never been a guard, guarding shit.

The rain began to sprinkle; thunder clapped in the distance behind us, the lightening confined to the clouds for the moment. However, once it began striking the ground, the flashing light would expose us like bank robbers dressed in sheets.

I said goodbye to the Lieutenant and Tate before heading out on my own; I found a ditch of sorts and made my way to the corner of the first hooch. I saw a guard tower with one guard in its top; he was looking into the sky at the coming weather. I spotted Joseph going up the ladder after him. I started toward the second tower when suddenly; a lone man emerged from the building next to the tower. I darted behind the corner of the structure and waited for him to come to me. However, just as he got to the end of the edifice, another man came out of the door behind him.

"Dut khoát, chó đi tiêu!" (Fucking dog shit!) He cursed, "Tôi se quay lai ngay ned." (I will be right back) he said going back inside.

While waiting for his return, his friend lit a cigarette standing with his back to me. I walked up behind him grabbing his chin with one hand and snapped his neck with the other. To conceal his body I picked him up and carried him behind the hooch laying him down quietly. Returning to my spot, I waited like a trap-door spider for the other one.

Joseph was coming down from the east tower heading for the south tower as Baker and Tate worked the other end of the village.

My man came back out of the hooch again looking for his friend. Not seeing his friend, he threw his hands up in disgust, and then began walking straight toward me. Just as he got to me, I stepped out in front of him. By the time he realized what I was, he, was dead. I placed his body with the other.

Higgins had found the officer quarters, however, there was only one person in the house. We had searched the other buildings walking among the sleeping who never knew that we were there. Still, these people were only regular Vietcong. There wasn't, any signs of other officers or Reyna.

Higgins and Joseph brought the single officer out of the building into the compound. He was unconscious. Joseph had him across his right shoulder wrapped in a blanket.

The rain is getting heavier at present; we had to decide what to do. If there was a facility for prisoner's here, we hadn't found it.

Tate appeared from the shadows. "There is a vent in the ground over there," he indicated.

All of us knew that meant tunnels; Higgins gave the order to kill the unconscious officer so Tate did.

Now separated once again, we spread out and began looking for a concealed entrance to the tunnels.

Working my way northeast, I tripped a Trip Flare. (A ground flare triggered by a trip wire used to signal and illuminate the night sky). It lit up exposing me as bright as day. With the light came an alarm!

The rest of the team managed to find cover while a single guard screamed over a loud speaker.

"Dung Lai! Dung Lai! (Stop! Stop!)

Before I could move, I had five of the little bastards all over me; I had no options but to give up my weapon. More of the black pajama, wearing bastards came out of the barracks. I had rapidly managed to become the evening's main attraction! To make matters worse, they were finding their dead sprinkled across the compound and were beginning to get excited about it.

The door opened to the officer quarters and a woman dressed in black came down the steps and walked directly toward me. From the same building, that Higgins had cleared only minutes before. As the woman came closer, the light from the parachute flares was fading. Nonetheless, there was still enough light to see. It was a woman in deed, and not just any woman. A shock went through my entire being. It was Ha`ng, the village girl from the highlands.

"Ha`ng?"

"Sergeant Logan," her hand on the butt of her holstered weapon. "We meet again."

"I don't understand."

"Mang lai cho anh!" (Bring him!) She said turning aside.

The rain had turned into a downpour, the lighting flashed all around us, the thunder was deafening.

We entered the officer quarters with the three of her men guarding me. Once inside I turned and grabbed one of the weapons from the man next to me. Another jammed the muzzle of an AK deep into my ribs; I twisted it out of his hands and rendered him unconscious. While holding the cocked AK to the first man's temple, "Where is she?" I demanded.

"Very good SGT. Logan, very well executed. I would hate to kill you so soon. I do so enjoy the torture of another human more than I can say," speaking up. "I trust you are speaking of the American nurse?"

"Where is she?"

"Dead if you don't release my man and sit down. Of course the choice is yours," smirking. Waving a finger at me and twisting her head. "My men have a party planned for her later. Lieutenant Nurse Reyna Hawks, I believe. You see, we will sell her with the collection of other pretty girls we have collected from various villages. She and the others will be sold in China to the highest bidder; the American beauty will bring a small fortune."

One of her men came into the hooch, walked over to her whispering in her ear. Staring at him, "Tat ca moi nguoi là đe tìm kiem toàn bo dien tích, tiêu diet bat ky ke xâm nhap ban tìm thay. Đe lai bon ve si o đây." (Everyone is to search the entire area, kill any intruders you find. Leave four-guards here).

The guard nodded then turned and walked back out again.

"I see you have been busy; you managed to kill twenty-six of my men. Of course you are operating alone, or did you bring friends?"

"I'm alone."

"If that's true, then I am a virgin, maybe I should wear white more often? But then again, we'll see."

I let go of the guard as the other two got up from the floor tending to their wounds. "Tìm kiem ông ta, ky luong!" (Search him, thoroughly!).

They found my seven knives I had hidden and my three grenades on my belt piling them in the center of the table. If alone, I would have tried taking matters in my own hands as trained to do. I was counting on the rest of the team to do their job. The gooks searching for them would not have a chance. I was hoping I would have enough time to stall the situation and give Higgins enough time to come for me.

Using only her hand, she dismissed all three guards.

"Care for some tea?" As she pulled a chair from under the table twisting its seat toward me, "Please, sit." Standing she poured tea for the both of us then moved to my side taking a chair.

Sitting, I had to ask. "Aren't you afraid I might try something?"

"I'm sorry, I thought you already did?" she pronounced. "I'll take that weapon please," she added holding out her hand. Her hair hung down her back. Her face had just enough makeup to cover any light lines she may have had. Her lips painted a light red. The black pajama top cut just low enough to show off the tops of her breast. Taking the AK from me, "You and I had a moment back there in the mountains, do you remember?" Sliding the chair closer, "Too bad we did not act upon our sexual urges at the time. Neither of us knowing anything about the other, you playing the hero with me playing the vixen, it could have been animalistic." Taking a sip of tea sitting the cup back down, "I have never had sex with an American, I wanted to when I was in the States, but never did."

"You surprise me, you were stateside?"

"Oh yes," she said, "I will tell you a story. When I was eighteen, they sent me to America to learn the language and culture; I attended Texas State College at night studying Business Administration and Language. From there I went to China where I studied the Art of War under General Chi Ho Dun. I was twenty-three by the time I returned to Vietnam."

"You've been busy, I'm curious, and what did you do before college?"

"Wow, let us see if I can say this without sounding as though I am a candidate for Saint-Hood. I think I was ordained to walk in the paths of allegiance to my country; I already had the courage to fight for it. My ancestors fought the French, the Chinese, the Japanese, and now the Americans. We won then just as we will win now. We are committed to paying the ultimate price for what we want, a united Vietnam. The Americans are committed only to failure. Your leaders are turning the United States into a pussy whipped world. You cannot fight a war by letting cowards protest a war while hiding behind symbols of Peace and empty words."

"Interesting."

"I do not include you or your kind in my statement, you are part of the group we call The Fog Killers. To capture one alive is truly a great thing. I think I will explore those sexual urges with you before my men enjoy seeing just what makes you tick. That is, when the time comes. Your kind doesn't have the courage to fight a man face to face; you have to hide in the dark like a thief in the night. Fog Killers are the thief's of life, a thief of spirits of men better than you."

Taking a drink of the tea, "This is very good."

"To continue my theory about the American's you are a taker of life as I am, but most of your compatriots pray to their God asking to be. Wounded so they can be, sent home, because of the cowards they are. They shoot themselves for the same purpose," she stared. "Your commanders in Washington, their hearts and souls are not in it, they let the politics decide how wars are to be fought." She stammered. "Flower Power, Black Power, and protest, your Black soldiers in Vietnam are not respected and called niggers, the Vietnamese people would never do that. They are tortured and killed in the United States just because they are Black and your law does nothing prevent it. Yet they fight for their country. Your Government sees this war as something they have to do to keep the economy going. None of those people are like us; we see war as something we love."

"I see," letting her rant.

"When I was twelve years old I became a woman. I was, trained by the best, just as you were, and like you, they taught me how to kill. When I was seventeen, they put me in command of a band of men which would follow me to your hell if need be. Like you, we hid in the shadows and undergrowth, knowing that we were in complete control. We have a lot in common you and me."

"I feel sorry for you?"

"And why is that?" Her face relaxed, her demeanor changing.

"When I saw you in the highlands for the first time, I perceived you to be this little girl of whom someone had taken advantage of. A girl who needed to be loved and cared for. You had just lost your sister and you looked as if though your heart had been wounded."

"You are so foolish; you wanted to be my knight in shining armor, and as a result I let you. Probably the product of too many Walt Disney Movies, as then and now, you think by complimenting a woman, they will throw their legs open and let you take them."

I didn't answer.

"You are caring, your charm and compliments will be your downfall. By the way, the girl back there in the highlands was not my sister. I never knew her. I dressed as a villager to find out who the village Chief was. They told us that he was giving the Americans information about our movements and weaponry. I spoke in Vietnamese to make them think I was one of them. Remember the Captain I shot?"

I nodded yes.

"I was in charge, he was my second in command, and his life bought the trust I needed from you. Thus, you let us to leave; you were my accomplice without knowing it. Thank you for allowing me to carry out my mission. All of those villagers you think you saved? We killed them and their Chief on the way back to our home."

"Why are you telling me all of this?"

"Why, not? Your fate is sealed, you will never tell anyone," pouring herself another cup of tea. "Would you like another?"

"I am surprised that Col. Tet isn't here, I thought he would in charge of this region; that is why I was surprised to see you here in his place."

Her eyes were ablaze. "Col Tet takes orders from me!"

"As true as that may be, Col. Tet is a man, and as you know, men are respected more than women," trying to get a rise out of her. "Col. Tet has taken credit for the success of Operations Dragon Fly, and Moon Beam, as recently as just two months ago."

"That's a lie; Gen. Tet was in Da Nang screwing bar girls while my men and I were putting our lives on the line! The man is a pig! He did not know of those operations until they were over!"

As I had hoped, her speech had changed; she was quickly becoming intimated and mad. "It's because you're a woman, some men refuse to believe a woman can accomplish the things that you claim you have."

"Enough! Bao ve!" (Guards!), bouncing to her feet as if her ass was on fire.

When the guards came in they grabbed me, then forced me through what I thought would be the back door. Instead, it was a door leading down into the tunnels that we had searched for but couldn't find. The tunnels had been here since Frances occupation. There was barracks with at least a hundred bunk beds down there, but they were all empty. We passed a large kitchen and a dining area as they led me to the cells dug out of the walls. The passage way was up to three meters wide in some areas. The upper crust was at least three to four meters thick. You could drive a tank over it, and it wouldn't fall in.

The cell doors were made of thick heavy Teak wood. We stopped in front of the second cell; one of the guards opened it. The guard behind me struck me in the back of the head with his rifle butt sending me across the room. I hit the wall sticking to it for a moment, trying to regain my senses. Both of them came at me, one of them slamming the muzzle of his weapon into my stomach again, I went down. Then they tied me to the bed in a sitting position. I was hoping Higgins and the others were about to act, because I had a feeling that time was running out.

"You soon die like dog," the guard said looking at me as he backed away locking the cell door behind him.

"Mang lai cho cô ay!" (Bring her!) Ha`ng ordered.

The guards went down the aisle where I heard Reyna screaming and yelling at them as they removed her from her cell. They responded by hitting and slapping her!

"Easy on the merchandise," Ha`ng ordered as they brought Reyna to her.

As Reyna passed my cell, I could see she still had her clothes on. She's dressed in a pair of black slacks with a white blouse that was tattered and torn with holes at the knees, looking as if she had been dragged. The left sleeve on her blouse was missing; her face bruised around her right cheek, her hair hung wildly down her back. The guard stopping in front of Ha`ng with Reyna at his side, her hands tied behind her back.

Ha`ng grabbed her by the hair pulling her face in close, first biting her lip, she then kissed Reyna on the mouth. Reyna squirmed and pulled back trying to get away, and spit in Hang's face.

Ha`ng wiped the liquid off her cheek with her hand, and licked it off her fingers. Smiling, "The taste of my enemy is sweet," and then turned to the guards. "Enjoy yourselves, but do not harm her any further unless the Sergeant tries something stupid. I want my turn with her before we dispose of her," turning and going back the way we had come.

The guards removed the ropes from Reyna's hands and then started tearing at her clothing. Ripping and cutting them from her body while she screamed crying out in protest. Nude, they forced her into the cell next to me than began strapping her to the bed spread eagle.

"Reyna! Look at me!" I screamed.

They strapped her legs to the bed tying them down on either side. Her screams of... "Stop! Don't do this!" Went unheard.

The first guard took off his boots and pants then got on top of her. She was going crazy trying to do what she could to fight him.

"Reyna! Look at me!" Again, screaming as loud as I could.

Looking at me through the bars, I could see the terror in her eyes as the guards began having their way with her.

"Look, at me baby, just keep looking at me!"

We were both crying as the other guard opened my cell door striking me in the head with the butt of his rifle; blood began streaming down my face.

Reyna, screaming curse words at the top of her voice.

Then I saw Higgins and the others coming down the steps at the end of the hall.

Tate took the guard who had hit me snapping his neck like a twig. The guard assaulting Reyna clambered to his feet as Higgins shot him in the head. Baker and Higgins untied Reyna first and then me. Joseph had gone to find some clothes for Reyna.

"Where's Ha`ng?" I asked

"The bitch is sipping wine with her ancestors," Baker said untying me...

I went to Reyna taking her into my arms, "I love you baby, I love you," kissing her face. She was so scared. Trembling and shaking, fear had completely overtaken her. She was crying uncontrollably. I just held her in my arms all the time trying to let her know everything was all right.

Once Joseph had returned with some clothes that he found in Hang's closet, I said, taking the clothes from Joseph, "Guy's give us a minute will yah?"

As they left, "Reyna honey, we gotta get out of here! Here put these on." Helping her with the pants, then held the shirt for her, they were both brown, which would blend into the background on the way home. Joseph had done well.

"I was so scared," she cried.

"I know, I know, but it's over! We've got to go, ok?" Holding to her face, she nodded in agreement, and then I gave her a kiss. "Here, put on your shoes."

* * * *

The trip back:

As we moved, everyone attended to Reyna's needs as they arose. It was as if she's our child and our fatherly instincts had kicked in, she moved with us as well as she could. They had her for almost five days depriving her of food and water, and feeding her a small portion once a day.

There were other girls in those cells. However, there was too many for us to safely, take with us. We would send in the Marines to rescue and care for them.

It was daylight now and we had been walking for almost an hour. We were moving slowly, searching the area for booby-traps as we went. We heard the dreaded Vietcong all around us, so being quiet and moving silently had become a necessity.

Higgins carried the radio; we had to find a secure place to call for an extraction and rescue of the imprisoned girls.

Moving into a thick area of undergrowth, we saw a band of Marines in the distance. They had their hands full fighting with the Vietcong on the other side of the riverbank.

There was a large clump of Nipa Grass floated in the narrow river inlet in front of me, and then I noticed a rifle barrel sticking out of it. Chuck was picking his targets, firing when he was sure that he was, locked on. We had heard Sniper Fire earlier, but until right now, we didn't know where it was coming from.

I pointed to Higgins giving a hand signal toward the water, joining me; we slowly approached the floating chunk of dirt and grass. Via my K-9, I emptied it into the dirt moving it in a circle as I fired. Blood began mixing with the river water as the clump of dirt slowly floated away.

"Sneaky sonofabitch," Higgins complained.

I went to check on Reyna, she was setting on the ground with her feet curled under her. She was not crying, but her eyes were still swollen and red.

I sat next to her, took some food and water out of my pack, and gave it to her.

"Thank you," she said.

"Shuuuu," I returned, leaning to her ear whispering. "They will hear us," meaning Charlie.

She nodded. I took a clean cloth from my medical pack, went to the river's edge and wet it and returned to her, tenderly I cleaned her face, and then put a bandage on her chin.

Going back to her ear, "I have been so stupid; I love you with all of my heart."

She looked at me, and then whispered into my ear, "Took you long enough."

Back to her ear, "Not really, I have loved you from the first time I met you."

The Mekong Delta area wasn't a jungle area as such; there were not areas of total coverage where we could travel by day without being seen.

The Mekong Delta covers an area of almost twenty-five-thousand square miles. The river crosses Cambodia and splits into nine tributaries known as River of Nine Dragons, nourishing thousands of rice paddies before making its way to the South China Sea.

The only real thing we had going for us was a General of ours, whom the Vietnamese called, *The Butcher of the Delta*. His policies were, *if it's Vietnamese and moving, shoot it!* He scared the hell out of the Vietcong.

Joseph was, assigned to Recon the upper riverbank to see what was up there, but had not returned yet. Baker and Tate were making sure the immediate area around us was secure.

Higgins moved in, whispering. "What do you think; want to chance Peaches coming in for an extraction?"

"I'm for it, Yessir."

"Check on SGT. Sacks, he's overdue, I'll key up the radio."

"Yessir."

Leaving my pack behind, I checked the clip in my K-9. I started out for Joseph with Reyna giving me a hug, and telling me to be careful.

As I traveled, I hunkered over checking for anything out of the ordinary as I moved. I stayed away from the riverbanks knowing they, were heavily mined and I had to be careful of not getting too bold in my movements. In the distance, I could hear and see at least thirty to forty-helicopters firing and buzzing around over a clearing. A massive Dust Off was under way; something big was going on, (Dust Off, a military term for air ambulance Medevac). As it was called, they were flying in under fire to pick the wounded in an attempt to transport them to an M*A*S*H Unit, placing them in harms-way. Ultimately, I had caught up with Joseph; he was behind a bush watching it all.

"Joseph!" He turned. "Let's go home." I said.

He fell in on me, and we started back. It wasn't long after that we reached the others.

"Peaches, is on the way." Higgins said finishing off a chocolate bar.

Reyna came to me, clinging to me like glue. I was expecting Lt. Higgins to say something about it since she was still a lieutenant. However, being the man he was, he never said a word.

"Sir," I said. "There's a massive operation going on north of here, hopefully it will cover Peaches arrival."

Higgins agreed.

We did not have to wait long before we heard Peaches coming in low from the north. Getting on the helicopter with the fastest of efficiency would be our primary goal. Every second he was in the air, he would be visible.

Peaches traveling fast brought the chopper in low, and then made a hard right. At that point, he came right for us! Stopping in mid-air, the chopper floated over the land like a large bug. We began running for it, I had Reyna with me, I was determined to make sure she got aboard first, and then here it came. A mortar hit just behind us, and as I turned, I saw Joseph's body explode into a large red shower of blood! His bones and shrapnel from the mortar shell tore into my body and face! I went down. Then another landed in front of the chopper sending debris everywhere. Tate and Baker grabbed me and rolled my body up onto the metal floor of the chopper. All aboard except for Joseph, Peaches pulled us up trying to get us out of there. A large black man was at the M-60 serving as door gunner. I looked for Jewels, but didn't see him. Small arms fire was hitting the chopper, and then I witnessed smoke coming from the engine. The engine started spitting and sputtering with Peaches fighting the controls. We were at fifteen-hundred feet when the final blow came. An RPG, (Rocket Propelled Grenade) took out our tail-rotor; the transmission coming apart like two-dollar suit. I was, thrown against the Plexiglas window knocking out most of the teeth on the right side of my mouth.

I remember seeing the earth coming up at us. Suddenly, I hit the ground unaware of what was going on around me. Unexpectedly the large black man that operated the M-60 had me up in his arms dragging me away from the burning chopper. Dropping me off in the brush he darted away to help someone else.

*150,000 Leonid meteors an hour visible
in the skies across the United States
Armed Forces Radio
17th Aug 1966*
Old news from a current program,
anything about the stars and space
intrigued me. Aired again on 01/02/67.

CHAPTER SEVENTEEN

SAYING GOODBYE: AS my eyes opened. I realized I was on the hospital ward with twin IV's pumping Saline and Antibiotics into my arms. There is a pair of lieutenant bars laying on the nightstand beside my bed and a carton of chocolate milk on ice. For a second I was wondering if I had been, promoted, which was short lived.

It was at that moment, the thoughts of Joseph came crashing in. My eyes began swelling with tears. I had not had time to process his death, we had shared everything since we were just kids, and the hurt of his death was just beginning to run long and deep.

"Good morning," Major Baginski said walking up on me. "I am sorry about SGT. Sacks; I know how close you two were. You guys were like brothers."

"He was a brother," trying to fight back the tears. "I am going to miss him."

Lt. Higgins, Tate, and Baker joined the Major. Tate and Baker were beat to hell; both of them were, bandaged in different areas on their bodies, Baker stood with a cane in his right hand.

"Where's Reyna?" I managed to ask.

"Sorry Jack, she didn't make it," Baker moaned.

I turned to the nightstand and picked up the lieutenant bars, "Are these, hers?"

"They are," Baginski, answered. "The milk is something she would have us do for you. It was Sgt. Baker's idea since she isn't here to do it herself."

Holding to her lieutenant bars, I closed my hand around them, and held them over my heart. I was overwhelmed with grief, "What happened to her?"

No one wanted to say it.

Raising my voice, "What happened to her?"

"She was ejected from the helicopter," Higgins sighed. "As you were when it went down."

"And Peaches?"

"He made it," Baginski said. "He's in, ICU, in a coma for now, but at least he's alive."

"What about the guy who pulled me out?"

"That would be SGT. Jamal, he made it." Tate spoke up.

"I'm sorry guys, but I would like to be alone."

Baginski to the others, "You heard the man," his hands up, "Let's give him some room."

They wished me well as they started toward the main entrance.

"SGT. Baker!" I called out.

Baker, broke rank and came to my side, I waited while the others cleared out before saying it. "I need your weapon," looking at his side arm.

"I can't do that," he said.

"I would do it for you," staring at him.

"Man, don't put this shit on me, not like this! I can't do it; you're my teammate, my friend for Christ's sake!"

Holding out my hand, "Pleaseee, give me your weapon!"

Reluctantly, Baker removed his .45 from its holster and handed it to me butt first. I checked the ammo clip to make sure it was loaded, then pumped a round into the chamber and placed it at my side with the safety off.

"Man, don't do this!" He pleaded.

"I've lost everything. Nothing matters to me anymore. What is the difference if I pull the trigger or not? I wanna see what's next! Who, fuckin' cares?"

"I know you're hurting, man. I know that, you've been through a lot, but we all have. We lost them too; it wasn't just you who has lost people you care about!"

Baker, the Rock as I had called him on many occasions started crying. "Now you want to take yourself out! That is one more loss for us! We care about you bro, you must know that!"

Finished he came to my bedside, sitting down next to me. Wrapping his big arms around me he hugged me as we both sat there crying like two small children in the dark.

* * * *

It was six days later before I could walk; Joseph and Reyna's coffins were sealed and sent stateside for the burial at Mountain View Baptist Church where we had attended as kids. I would not be there for their funerals, but I would-be there eventually. My first tour in Da Nam will be over in just two short weeks.

Baker wants me to sign up for another tour. Then, he wants to go home, back to Alabama to check on his family. He does not want me to be alone because he doesn't trust my emotions. He believes I will hurt myself if given the chance. I seriously thought about it, but I am not going to do that. I will admit that it was my first thought waking up in the hospital to find everyone gone. I also thought about going home; it's time to end the madness I have let myself fall. I was thinking that there had to be more to life than this. However, seriously thinking about it, I realized that I loved the action. I was addicted to the adrenaline rush of it all. If I went home how I would never fit in. I would never be able to speak of the atrocities I have committed. No way would people ever understand. I found comfort in talking it over with God, but since it was a one-way conversation, I was, left to figure things out on my own...

* * * *

Early on, the seventh day, Baker and I volunteered for another tour with an immediate thirty-day leave.

Standing at Maya's gravesite with Peaches, who was a little battered and wounded, but well. Actually, I was there just to say goodbye. Peaches realizing I needed a moment, decided to let me have it. He and Baker went for a coffee saying they would be back...

I had visited Maya's grave every evening while I waited for the days to pass. I felt that I would be physically ready to go with Baker.

I brought Maya flowers and said prayers for her. I would never forget her.

Promised to think of Maya, Andy Layton, Joseph and my beloved Reyna as visions of them ran through my mind. Even though I did not know SGT. Hocus I will remember him for like Maya, he was a gentle soul. "Maya, Andy, Joseph, Reyna, and Hocus, Tam biet, Tôi yêu ban!" (Goodbye I love you!")...

Date, of last entry into my journal 01/19/67, I will keep these journals not knowing for sure just what to-do with them. Perhaps in time I will read them for the pleasant memories. Maybe I will burn them in an attempt to forget the bad memories and what has happened here, if nothing else, maybe they will serve a purpose not known to me as of yet, *Jack Logan*